NEW Literacy Kit

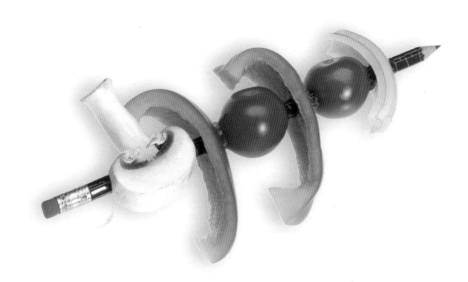

YEAR 7

Geoff Barton

OXFORD
UNIVERSITY PRESS

OXFORD
UNIVERSITY PRESS

Great Clarendon Street, Oxford OX2 6DP

Oxford University Press is a department of the University of Oxford.
It furthers the University's objective of excellence in research,
scholarship, and education by publishing worldwide in

Oxford   New York

Auckland   Cape Town   Dar es Salaam   Hong Kong   Karachi
Kuala Lumpur   Madrid   Melbourne   Mexico City   Nairobi
New Delhi   Shanghai   Taipei   Toronto

With offices in

Argentina   Austria   Brazil   Chile   Czech Republic   France   Greece
Guatemala   Hungary   Italy   Japan   Poland   Portugal   Singapore
South Korea   Switzerland   Thailand   Turkey   Ukraine   Vietnam

Oxford is a registered trade mark of Oxford University Press
in the UK and in certain other countries

British Library Cataloguing in Publication Data

Data available

ISBN-13: 978-0-19-832171-2
ISBN-10: 0-19-832171-6

10 9 8 7 6 5 4 3 2 1

Printed in Italy by Rotolito Lombarda.

Assembled by ZED, Oxford.

P16 Alamy Images; **p17** Alamy Images; **p21** Photodisc/OUP; **p27** Capital
Pictures; **p29** Ronald Grant Archive; **p30** Universal Pictorial Press; **p31t** Capital
Pictures; **p31bl&r** Universal Pictorial Press; **p33** Eye Ubiquitous; **p34** Alex
Hibbs/OUP; **p38** Stockbyte; **p40** Stapleton Collection/Corbis; **p41** Mary Evans
Picture Library; **p30** Stockbyte/OUP; **p48** Alex Hibbs/OUP; **p51** Universal
Pictorial Press; **p52** Mary Evans Picture Library; **p53** Mary Evans Picture Library;
p54 Alex Hibbs/OUP; **p61** Alamy Images; **p65** Jane Alexander/Photofusion; **p68**
Alamy Images; **p75** Zefa-Madison/Powerstock; **p79** Topham/Picturepoint; **p80**
Alex Hibbs/OUP; **p81** OUP, **p82** Eye Ubiqitous; **p84** Stockbyte/OUP; **p87**
Photonica; **p89** Christa Stadler/Photofusion; **p91** Photographers Library; **p92t**
Alex Hibbs; **p92b** Sony; **p99** Superstock; **p101** OUP; **p103t** Alex
Macnaughton/Rex Features; **p103b** Random House Group Ltd; **p104l** Michael
Taylor/OUP; **p106** Alex Macnaughton/Rex Features; **p108** Alamy Images; **p109**
Alamy Images; **p117** Alamy Images; **p118b** Corel Professional Photos/OUP; **p121**
OUP; **p122** Photodisc/OUP; **p123** OUP; **p124** OUP; **p126** Rex Features; **p128**
OUP; **p131** Richard Young/Christopher Little; **p132** Sipa Press/Rex Features;
p134 Topham Picturepoint; **p136** Alex Hibbs/OUP; **p139** Topham Picturepoint;
p142 OUP; **p143** OUP; **p145** Eye Ubiquitous; **p148** John Cleare/Mountain
Camera; **p153** OUP; **p161l&r** Capital Pictures; **p164** Ronald Grant Archive;
p168 Ronald Grant Archive; **p171** Mary Evans Picture Library; **p173** Capital
Pictures.

Illustrations are by Andy Hammond/Illustration Ltd: **p62**, **p118t**; Charles
Keeping Estate: **p169**; Peter Melnyczuk: **p141**, **p150**; Vincent Vingla/Illustration
Ltd: **p11**.

Cover photograph: Mark Mason/OUP

ACKNOWLEDGEMENTS

Crown Copyright material, extract from leaflet: 'Mobile Phones and Health'
(Department of Health), is reproduced under Class Licence Number
C01P0000148 with the permission of the Controller of HMSO and the Queen's
Printer for Scotland.

We are also grateful for permission to reprint the following copyright material:

Joan Aiken: extract from 'Something' in *A Fit of Shivers* (Victor Gollancz, 1990),
copyright © Joan Aiken Enterprises Ltd 1990, reprinted by permission of A M
Heath & Co Ltd on behalf of Joan Aiken.

BBC: extract on 'Mobile Phones' from *BBC Newsround* website, 20.7.00, reprinted
by permission of the BBC, www.bbc.co.uk.

The Bristol Group Ltd: advertisement for the 'Barlow Knee Support'.

The Citizenship Foundation: extract from *Young Citizen's Passport* (2000), reprinted
by permission of Hodder and Stoughton Educational Ltd.

Pamela Coleman: extract from interviews about their first day at school first
published in *The Times Educational Supplement* 25.8.00, copyright © Pamela
Coleman 2000, reprinted by permission of the author.

Amanda Craig: 'Thrill to Manaxa; A choice of books for older readers', *The
Independent*, 15.4.01, copyright © The Independent 2001, reprinted by permission
of Independent Newspapers.

Roseanne Flynn: 'The City People Meet Themselves' from *Wondercrump Poetry!*
edited by Jennifer Curry (Red Fox, 1994), reprinted by permission of The
Random House Group Ltd.

Katharine Frazer-Barnes: 'Rules too tight for comfort', first published in *The Times
Educational Supplement* 5.11.99, copyright © Katharine Frazer-Barnes 1999,
reprinted by permission of the author.

David Gillard: 'My Kind of Day', interview with Millvina Dean, Survivor of the
Titanic, *Radio Times*, 23 December 2000–5 January 2001 reprinted by permission
of Radio Times, BBC Worldwide.

Mark Haddon: review from www.bookheads.org.uk published by permission of
Gillon Aitken Associates Ltd on behalf of the author and of Booktrust.

Susan Hill: extract from *The Mist in the Mirror* (Vintage), copyright © Susan Hill
1992, reprinted by permission of Sheil Land Associates Ltd on behalf of the
author.

Steve Moss (Ed.): from *The World's Shortest Stories* (Running Press, 1995), copyright
© 1998, 1995 by Steve Moss: 'Grandma Meets the Axe Murderer' by Diane Elliott
and 'Moment of Decision' by Tina Milburn, reprinted by permission of Running
Press Book Publishers, Philadelphia and London, www.runningpress.com.

Alfred Noyes: 'The Highwayman' from *Collected Poems* (John Murray, 1963),
reprinted by permission of The Society of Authors as the Literary Representative
of the Estate of Alfred Noyes.

Louise Osmond and Phil Cool: 'Let's Get Physical', *The Indy*, 5.10.89, copyright ©
The Independent 1989, reprinted by permission of Independent Newspapers.

J K Rowling: extract from *Harry Potter and the Chamber of Secrets* (Bloomsbury,
1998), copyright © J K Rowling 1998, reprinted by permission of Christopher
Little Literary Agency on behalf of the author.

Save the Children: advertisement 'Take Children Seriously'.

Keith Waterhouse: extract from *City Lights* (1994), reprinted by permission of
Hodder and Stoughton Ltd.

and Tom Fullam and Nick Vollmer for use of their student work.

We have tried to trace and contact all copyright holders before publication. If
notified the publishers will be pleased to rectify any errors or omissions at the
earliest opportunity.

Contents

Introduction

The New Literacy Kit has been written to build your skills in English, develop your self-confidence, and make you an expert in working with a range of different texts. This new edition provides starters, texts, activities and assessment tasks which will help you to see what you are doing well and what you need to work on.

The Year 7 Students' Book combines texts from the three writing triplets:

- Inform, Explain, Describe
- Persuade and Analyse
- Imagine, Explore, Entertain

These are based on the national curriculum for English (though we have linked persuade and analyse together to build your understanding of them). By grouping texts like this, you will be able to develop a deeper understanding of the way different text types work. This is essential preparation for helping you to write in a range of styles and across your different subjects at school.

As always in English, these categories will often overlap, but knowing that you are covering all parts of the English curriculum will help to build your confidence.

This is how each unit is organized:

Starters

Each unit has a starter activity. Starters are great fun because they get your brain working. They lead you into a topic with lively, often unexpected tasks, which tend to involve minimum writing and maximum thinking. Use these activities to loosen your brain up, practise your teamwork, and feel your way into the main topic of the unit.

Learning objectives

The learning objectives help to map out the learning journey ahead of you. They don't tell you what you will do but what you will learn. That's really important - having a clear sense from the beginning of what you are expected to learn.

Introduction

This briefly sets the scene for each text, tuning you into the context of the material and helping you to know when it was written, by whom, and for what purpose. The more we know about texts in advance, the better prepared we are for discussing, understanding and exploring them. In this section, you may be asked to think about questions or ideas before reading the texts, or to make predictions about what might happen in them.

To do well in English, you need to have an understanding of why you are reading a text and how it relates to other texts you know. The introductions are designed to help you build this understanding.

Texts and activities

The texts have been carefully selected to interest and entertain you, and to help develop your knowledge of different text types. They are followed by questions, tasks and activities which are grouped in three ways:

♦ First, there are questions about understanding the text. These should build your confidence quickly by allowing you to spot key features and to show that you understand what the text is about.

♦ Next, you are asked questions about interpreting the text. These questions are more open-ended. They give you a chance to explore your own responses and to give your own opinion.

♦ Finally, there is a section on language and structure, which is a key part of your work in English. The work you do with language and structure will help you to become familiar with the language choices that writers make, and allow you to explore details at word, sentence and text level.

Writing activity

You can develop your understanding of the text further in the writing activity. It encourages you to see things from the point of view of the writer - testing out ideas, writing creatively and reflecting on your own language decisions.

Extended writing

Each unit gives you an opportunity to put into practice the skills you have learned earlier on. You'll be able to practise structuring your ideas, linking words and sentences, choosing the right vocabulary and making the right impact on your reader. The extended task always builds on the skills you have covered in the unit, so you should feel a real sense of making progress.

Assess your learning

This section helps you to review your own progress - not through formal tests and exams, but by helping you to evaluate your development against the learning objectives of the unit.

Speaking and listening

To make progress in English, speaking and listening are an essential lesson ingredient. In *The New Literacy Kit*, listening and speaking are built in, from starter activities to assessment. In the process you should develop a better understanding of your own skills and qualities in speaking and as a listener.

Above all, *The New Literacy Kit* has been designed as a lively and thought-provoking resource that helps you to make real progress in English. I hope you enjoy using it.

Geoff Barton

Inform, Explain, Describe

Getting started
Unit 1   Information texts

Every day we are bombarded with information – from the TV, Internet, signs, noticeboards and so on.

1 Using a spider diagram, note down the sources of information you have seen since you got up this morning.

2 Use different shapes to show the importance of each source of information. Draw the shape next to each one.

Information that it was essential to know   *Information that was useful but not essential to know*   *Information that you really didn't need to know*

3 Now think about which source of information uses the most **formal** language and which uses the most **informal** language. Underline the most formal source with a zigzag line, and draw stars around the most informal one, like this:

4 a Compare with other students how much information you have received today and how much of it was essential, useful or unnecessary.

b Look at which source of information in your class was the most formal and which was the most informal (and how you could tell).

Unit 2   Recounts

How good are you at telling stories – either about your own experiences, those of other people or invented characters?

On the next page is the opening of a story. Working with a partner or in a small group, take it in turns to add the next stage of the story. To make this more challenging, use the connectives from column A or B to link the ideas together.

As the boy walked past the abandoned warehouse, he paused …

A	B
because	and
then	next
whilst	as
much later	and so
despite this	after that
finally	although
	earlier

Unit 3 Explanation texts

1 You want to explain the topics below. For each topic, choose the text type on the right which would be most suitable for explaining it.

Topic	Text type
1 why volcanoes erupt	**a** website
2 how to look after a rabbit	**b** text message
3 a guide to the Houses of Parliament	**c** leaflet
4 advice on how to revise for exams	**d** poster
5 how much fat is in a breakfast cereal	**e** information book
6 how to protect your dog from rabies	**f** packaging on a product
7 explain to young children not to talk to strangers	**g** factsheet
	h story

2 Now choose the text type that would be most *unsuitable*. Try to explain why.

Unit 4 Instruction texts

Some friendly aliens have just arrived on Earth. They have many questions for Earthlings:

* How do I send a text message?

* How do I get from this room to school reception?

* How do you human beings clean your teeth?

Working with a partner, your task is to give detailed instructions to the aliens, but you must not use your hands to add gestures, or use fillers like 'er' and 'um'.

1 Sit facing your partner, clasp your hands together, and take turns at giving an explanation.

2 After doing this a few times, discuss the challenge. What are three secrets of giving a successful explanation without using gestures or fillers?

Unit 5   Descriptive texts

For this activity, use your English exercise book (turned face down) or a textbook. Your challenge is to use your descriptive powers to get to know your book, so that when it is put in the middle of a table with lots of others, you can identify it.

1 Spend *one minute* studying your book's shape, distinguishing marks, colour and special features.

2 Jot down the key features of your book.

3 Work in groups of three to four. Mix the books up and see if you can spot yours.

4 Now work in a larger group and mix the books up again. Describe your book to someone else in the group. See if he or she can identify it from your description.

What are information texts?

Purpose and audience

Information texts need to be clear and easy to understand. Their audience might know nothing about a topic and want to learn (for example, 'A Beginner's Guide to Playing the Guitar'); or they may already know something about the topic but need more detail (for example, 'The Advanced Guide to Website Design').

Text level features

Information texts often contain complex information and must present it as clearly as possible. This may mean using a range of **layout features**. You might expect to find:

◆ headings and sub-headings

◆ short paragraphs

◆ different font styles, bold and italic print

◆ bullet points

◆ diagrams.

The sequence of information will be important. The text may start with **general statements**, followed by more **detail** later. **Examples** will often be included.

Sentence level features

Information texts are often written in the **present tense** ('Diet *is* an important concern …'). They may use an impersonal style, with the **third person** ('Diet is …') rather than first or second person ('I think …' or 'You should …').

Information texts will often use **connectives** to help the reader follow the organization of ideas – for example, *then, so, next*.

Word level features

Information texts may use **technical terms** and complex language if appropriate. Generally these texts will use vocabulary which gives facts rather than a lot of description.

Formal writing
Young Citizen's Passport

Learning objectives

With this extract we examine a text that gives information in an organized way. These are the objectives you will be studying:

- Word level: develop your use of link words and phrases

- Sentence level: become more skilful in managing tenses

- Reading: evaluate sources of information; identify the main ideas in a text; explore the way media texts are tailored to their audience; study the way print, sound and image help to create meaning; explore the features of non-fiction texts

- Writing: organize texts appropriately; select and present information well

- Speaking and listening: listen for and recall the main points

Introduction

This text is aimed at young people and aims to inform them about their rights and responsibilities. Explore the way it presents the information. When you have studied this text, you will have a chance to write an information text of your own. If possible, start by reading the questions in 'Understanding the text', then listen to the text being read aloud. This will help you to listen for clues about how the text has been organized.

young citizen's **passport**

Part-time work

At what age?

The law controlling the work of young people below school leaving age varies from one town or country to another. Under the *Children and Young Persons Act 1933*, each local authority creates its own by-laws giving the terms and conditions for the employment of young people in that area.

Employment rights

In 1994, senior judges decided that UK laws unfairly discriminated against part-time workers. As a result, many of the rights of those in part-time jobs (even if it's for only a couple of hours per week) are the same as those of people in full-time employment.

These state the kind of work that a young person may, or may not, do and require employers to inform the council of all young people they employ. Although largely ignored, the rules also state that, generally speaking, anyone below school leaving age who has a part-time job must have a medical certificate of fitness for work and an employment card issued by the local council.

The only kind of employment children under 14 can be given is occasional light farm work, supervised by a parent, or parts in plays or films, etc., for which a special licence is required from the local authority.

Children aged 14 or over may be employed only in light work approved by their local authority.

No young person below school leaving age may be employed before 7 a.m. or after 7 p.m., for more than one hour before the start of school, or for more than two hours on a school day, or on a Sunday.

New rules require a magistrates' licence for someone aged 14–16 to be paid to take part in sport.

There are few restrictions on the employment of 16 or 17 year olds. However, people under 18 cannot normally work in a bar, unless they work in a restaurant where drinks are served with meals, or are being trained for the licensing trade under a Modern Apprenticeship scheme. Copies of the by-laws controlling the employment of young people in your area can be obtained from the local library, council or education office. Information is also available from the Low Pay Unit.

A boy of 14, working in a factory making beds, suffered severe injuries when his arm was trapped in an unguarded machine. A court fined his employer £1,000 for failing to fit a guard to the machine and £200 for employing a child. The employer also paid £438 towards the cost of the case.

passport

UNDERSTANDING THE TEXT

1 What kind of work may children under the age of 14 legally do?

2 Is the age for starting work the same in all areas?

3 How long may a child under 16 work before the start of the school day?

4 In what kind of bar may people under 18 work?

INTERPRETING THE TEXT

5 An information text for young people should look lively and attractive. Look at the layout of the page. How has the designer tried to do this here? Say something about:

♦ the images

♦ the use of boxes and panels around text

♦ the choice of font styles.

6 Look at the first paragraph. What is the source of the facts about what the law says? How much can you 'trust' in what you have learned from this text? Does giving the source make the text feel reliable and factual? Write a brief paragraph explaining your response.

LANGUAGE AND STRUCTURE

1 Information texts can be written in the third person, like this:

No young person below school leaving age may be employed …

They can also be written in the second person, like this:

If you are below school leaving age, you may not be employed …

Choose one paragraph and rewrite it using the second-person form. Does this make it sound more personal? Write a sentence saying whether you think the text becomes more or less easy to follow as a result.

2 Information texts are usually written in the present tense. Find an example in this text of a sentence in the past tense. Say why this change of tense is necessary.

3 Information texts need to be clearly organized. How are different points linked together in this text? Write down three words or phrases which the writer uses to link ideas.

> ## Hint
> ● Linking words and phrases might include:
> *these, that, another, also, secondly, next.*

4 The writer of an information text often makes some general points and then backs them up with specific examples.

Use a table like this to show two examples of the way this writer supports ideas with examples. Fill in the missing information.

General point	Supporting example(s)
Only certain kinds of work are available for children under 14	
	People under 18 cannot normally work in a bar

WRITING ACTIVITY

Imagine you are working for a student advice service and you receive a letter asking for advice:

I am 13 and I wish to get a part-time job. I have been offered a paper round by my local newsagent. Am I allowed to take it and, if so, what hours am I allowed to work?

Duncan

Write a short information text for Duncan. It should cover the rules for employing young people which are relevant to his case. Remind yourself of the features of information texts, such as using the third person and the present tense. Your text should be clearly organized and give examples. Then write a brief letter to Duncan, explaining that you are enclosing this information sheet.

Informal writing
A Guide to Health

Learning objectives

This text is an example of information given in an informal, but well-organized, way. These are the objectives you will be studying:

- Word level: recognize areas of your own spelling that need developing; explore words in their context

- Sentence level: vary the formality of your writing according to audience and context

- Reading: locate information in texts; identify the main ideas in a text; explore the way media texts are tailored to their audience; study the way print, sound and image help to create meaning

- Writing: develop your drafting skills; organize texts appropriately; select and present information well

Introduction

This information text was created by Nick Vollmer, a Year 9 student, in his PSHE lessons. His class had been studying ways of staying healthy. His homework was to design a leaflet informing other students about eating healthily. When you have read his work, you will have the chance to present the information in a different way.

UNDERSTANDING THE TEXT

1 What are the four main types of foods?

2 Write down one tip that the writer gives for creating a balanced diet.

3 How much food does the average person eat in a lifetime?

4 What are micronutrients?

Nick Vollmer of W2

A GUIDE TO HEALTH

The Statistics

How much should we be eating?

- 25-30% of the food we eat should be FATS
- 15-20% of the food we eat should be PROTEIN
- 55-60% should be CARBOHYDRATE

Fun Facts

☺ In you're lifetime, you eat 100 tonnes of food

☺ Macronutrients means fats, protein, and carbohydrates

☺ Mircronutrients means vitimins & minerals

All Health

☢ You can be physically or mentally unhealthy

☢ Physically unhealthy is when you are e.i. over weight or on drugs

☢ To be mentally unhealthy is when e.i. you're stressed

Types of Food

This will help you to under stand what catagories foods come under

- **Carbohydrates**– Any foods containing wheat
- **Dairy**– Any foods or drink containing milk or butter
- **Meat, fish, protein**– Meats, fish, or foods containing protein
- **Fruit & Veggies**– apples, oranges, potatoes, etc.

A balanced Diet

✔ You should get 5-9 servings of carbs. a day

✔ 5-9 servings of friut and veggies a day

✔ Try to get 2-3 servings of dairy foods a day

✔ When you eat meat, fish, or protein, try to keep it in a low fat regoin. But try to get 2-3 servings a day

✔ Use fatty, sugary foods sparingly

Note: Use a variety of foods!!

INTERPRETING THE TEXT

5 If you had to pick out the three main ideas in the text, what would they be?

6 Information needs to be presented clearly. Nick Vollmer uses some diagrams (e.g. the pyramid) and some images (e.g. clip-art showing a pig on a bike). Which of his presentational devices do you think work best? Which would you have done differently?

7 The leaflet is aimed at students aged 11 to 14. How might the text have been different if it was aimed at:

   a an older audience (e.g. aged 35 to 50)

   b a younger audience (e.g. aged 9 to 11)?

LANGUAGE AND STRUCTURE

1 Look at the way the writer organizes his information. Compare the information he puts on each side of his leaflet by completing these sentences:

   a The first side of the leaflet gives information on …

   b The second side of the leaflet gives information on …

2 The writer uses a variety of sentence functions in the leaflet. Find an example of:

   ♦ a statement

   ♦ a question

   ♦ a command.

3 Nick Vollmer is writing for an audience aged 11 to 14. A good information text will use language to appeal to its age group. Find examples where Nick:

   ♦ uses headings to grab the reader's interest

   ♦ addresses the reader directly.

4 Information texts can include commands that directly address the reader. Look at the tone this writer uses when he gives commands. He could have said: 'Eat 2–3 servings of dairy foods a day'. This would sound impersonal and more like an order. How does he make his commands seem more personal and friendly?

5 Nick Vollmer's leaflet contains a number of spelling or typing errors. He uses a personal spelling notebook at school. Which words do you notice that he should add to his book and learn to spell accurately?

6 Imagine you are Nick Vollmer's teacher and you are marking his leaflet. What feedback would you give him? What do you think are his leaflet's strengths and weaknesses?

Writing as if you are his teacher, give him three brief comments on:

a the presentation of the leaflet

b the way he uses language

c ways to improve it.

You could also give him a grade or mark out of ten.

WRITING ACTIVITY

For some audiences you might want a leaflet to have a more formal, impersonal tone. You might want to emphasize the facts more, rather than the personal advice to the reader.

On one side of A4, use the information from Nick Vollmer's leaflet and present it in a more formal, impersonal way.

Try to:

◆ avoid addressing the reader directly

◆ avoid compressing words (e.g. say 'it is' rather than 'it's')

◆ avoid any comic or chatty details.

Quickly put together your leaflet. What kind of audience do you think it would be best suited to?

Extended writing

Very quickly, write down a list of points on one of the topics below. Don't try to organize them at all – just get down as many points as you can think of.

Topics

+ The way your school buildings are organized (information for a visitor)

+ A singer, group, or hobby that you know a lot about

+ A place you have visited (e.g. on holiday or a school trip)

As a homework activity, you could do some research on one of the topics so that you have more factual information.

Once you have gathered the information, create a short information text – for example, 'A Visitor's Guide to this School' or 'Essential Facts about Majorca'.

Working on your own, create an information text which:

+ uses the present tense

+ has an impersonal, factual tone

+ organizes the information you have collected in a way that is useful to the reader.

Then make up five factual questions about your information.

Read your information text to a partner, and then ask her or him to answer the questions. See how far he or she has followed the main points of your text. Ask for feedback about whether you could have made any of it clearer, and if so, how.

What are recounts?

Purpose and audience

Recounts are texts which tell us about events. They may be designed to inform us (such as, in a history textbook, a description of the build-up to a battle); or they may be more personal – a diary entry or autobiography describing an event in a person's life.

The audience may already be familiar with the topic or writer, or the information may all be new. The writer will usually structure his or her ideas in **chronological order** – that is, the events will be retold in the sequence in which they happened.

Text level features

Because they are usually chronological, most recounts will begin with an **opening paragraph** describing the setting or the start of the event; the **last paragraph** will usually be about the end of the event or its aftermath. Paragraphs in between will use **connectives** to link the sequence of ideas together.

Sentence level features

Recounts may use the **first person** (for stories and autobiography) or **third person** (for factual reports). They will usually use the **past tense**. There may be a variety of **sentence types** to hold the reader's interest. Short sentences may be used to build tension or suspense. Sometimes a writer may use **dialogue** to move the story forward or tell us more about a character.

Word level features

Recounts often aim to answer the questions: *who?, what?, when?, where?, why?* Writers paint pictures with words, so we may find descriptive writing, with techniques such as **similes** and **metaphors** used to create vivid images. Writers' choice of words may include the simple or complex, the formal or informal, depending on what they are aiming to achieve.

Autobiographical writing
Millvina Dean, Survivor of the Titanic

Learning objectives

With this extract, we will focus on the features of a personal recount, written informally. You will study these objectives:

- Word level: develop your use of link words and phrases

- Sentence level: become more skilful in managing tenses; increase the variety of sentences you use; vary the formality of your writing according to audience and context

- Reading: evaluate sources of information; identify the main ideas; infer and deduce meanings; explore writers' language choices

- Writing: develop your drafting skills; organize texts appropriately; improve your descriptive writing

Introduction

When the Titanic sank in 1912, more than 1,500 lives were lost. Nowadays, few of the survivors of the disaster are still alive. But here is one, Millvina Dean, thinking back (in a *Radio Times* article) about her life. When you have studied her recount, you can try writing one of your own.

Millvina Dean, Survivor of the Titanic

I can't bear ice in my drinks – it always makes me think of the iceberg, you see. I'm the youngest *Titanic* survivor – there are only five of us left – as I was nine weeks old when it sank in 1912, so obviously I can't remember anything about it. But my poor father drowned that day and whenever I imagine an iceberg I think of him. His body was never found – it may still be in the ship. I'm 88 and, latterly, the *Titanic* has totally changed my life.

Until a few years ago I was living quietly in retirement in the New Forest, but now much of my time is spent travelling all over the world to speak at conventions as a guest of the various *Titanic* societies. I'm an honorary member of eight – in Canada, America, two in Ireland, Scotland, France, Germany and here in England. Until the wreck was discovered there wasn't nearly so much interest in the disaster. My mother, who died in 1975, didn't tell me about what we'd been through until I was eight. She'd be absolutely amazed that I've become a sort of celebrity because of it.

My whole family – my father Bertram, my mother

Georgetta and my 18-month-old brother, Bertram Vere – was on that maiden voyage. We were going to start a wonderful new life in America – my father planned to open a tobacconist's shop in Kansas City. We travelled steerage – that's third class – and most of the third-class passengers were to die because they couldn't get from the lower decks to the lifeboats. I'm convinced that my father was a hero and that his quick response saved us. My mother was woken by a loud crash, and Father immediately told her to go to the lifeboats with the children. He kissed her goodbye and said he would see her later – but she never saw him again. I was bundled in a sack by a sailor and thrown into lifeboat 13. My mother followed but my little brother got separated from us and put in another lifeboat. We were all picked up by the *Carpathia*, but my dear father went down with the *Titanic*.

My mother, brother and I came back to Southampton, and I've spent all my life around the New Forest. I worked as a cartographer and a secretary and, once, as an assistant in a tobacconist's – I felt that Father would have approved. But I'd hardly given any thought to the *Titanic* when, in 1988, I was invited to attend a convention in Boston, and since then I haven't stopped. I've been to so many places that I would never otherwise have gone

to, and wherever I go people make a terrific fuss of me, which I like! And I don't mind travelling by boat – I've been on several cruises and even given a talk on the *QE2*.

I'm just back from attending the opening of an exhibition of *Titanic* artefacts in Stockholm, and now I'm off to Ireland for the opening of a restaurant named after the ship. I'm an honorary citizen of Regina, in Canada, and Kansas City, and I've been given a civic reception in Cobh in Ireland, where the *Titanic* docked before setting off for America. The local council here have even named a road after me – Millvina Close. And there are always dozens of letters from all over the world to answer. People just address them to Millvina Dean, *Titanic* survivor, Southampton – but they all arrive.

I'll be staying at home this Christmas, but I'd rather not watch the *Titanic* film. When panic sets in at the end I would be wondering about my father, and it would be too upsetting. But I have been invited to meet Kate Winslet and the director, James Cameron, and I've seen two Leonardo DiCaprio lookalikes at conventions. They were exactly like him. Very handsome.

Millvina Dean was talking to David Gillard

UNDERSTANDING THE TEXT

1 How many Titanic survivors were left at the time Millvina Dean gave her interview?

2 How old was she when the ship sank?

3 How many members of her family were on the Titanic and how many survived?

4 How is Millvina Dean still involved with the Titanic?

5 Why does she not wish to watch the film *Titanic*?

6 Summarize what you think are the three main points made in the text.

INTERPRETING THE TEXT

7 How reliable do you find Millvina Dean's account? Does her recount feel like a historical document, full of accurate facts? Say why or why not.

8 Write down one thing you learn about Millvina Dean's character from the text.

9 What is Millvina Dean's attitude to the celebrity status (fame) she has achieved? Do you think she welcomes the attention or does she try to avoid it? Write a short paragraph saying how you can tell.

Hint
- Look for a sentence where she says how she feels about people making 'a terrific fuss' of her.

LANGUAGE AND STRUCTURE

1 Look at the first sentence of the article.

   a Why do you think the writer chose this as the first sentence?

   b Do you think it is a good beginning for the article?

2 Look at the end of the first sentence, where the writer uses the phrase 'you see'. Does this phrase make the text seem:

more chatty   more formal   more informal   too relaxed   friendly
like a letter?

Choose the best description. Then write a sentence explaining your choice.

3 Recounts can use a wide range of sentences. Most of Millvina Dean's sentences are complex, e.g. 'We travelled steerage – that's third class – and most of the third-class passengers were to die because they couldn't get from the lower decks to the lifeboats.'

A few sentences are simple, e.g. 'They were exactly like him.'

Which of these statements do you think best describes the effect of this range of sentences? Choose the opening of the statement you most agree with, and then finish it off in your own words.

a The variety of sentences makes the text vivid because …

b The variety of sentences makes the text hard to follow because …

c The variety of sentences holds our interest because …

d The variety of sentences makes the text feel like a spoken account because …

4 How does the writer link the different ideas in the text together? Look for three words or phrases which help to do this.

5 Recounts are usually written in the past tense. Here, the writer describes the events of the Titanic using the past tense, and writes about her life now using the present tense. Find sentences which illustrate both tenses.

Past tense:

Present tense:

6 Although Millvina Dean's recount is not all in chronological order, some paragraphs *do* tell events in the order they happened. Which paragraphs do this?

7 At the end of the text it says 'Millvina Dean was talking to David Gillard'. In other words, the article is based on an interview. Yet it is written as if it were a personal account. Does this change your view on how valid or reliable the text is?

Write a sentence or two describing how you think the text has been written, and by whom.

8 Using the article you have read, complete this fact file about Millvina Dean:

Name:

Age:

Where she lives:

What she now does:

What she did earlier in her life:

What happened to her father:

What happened to her mother, her brother and herself on the Titanic:

How the Titanic disaster has affected her life positively and negatively:

What kind of person she is:

WRITING ACTIVITY

Take the facts from Millvina Dean's article, which you gathered for question 8 above. Think about a different way that they might be presented. Imagine you are writing an article about Millvina Dean for a local newspaper. Your focus is what happened on the Titanic, rather than her thoughts and feelings now. Your aim is to communicate to readers the panic and fear of the night the Titanic sank, and the way one survivor got free.

Aim to:

◆ write in the past tense

◆ structure the article chronologically (i.e. in the order events happened)

◆ use connectives (*then, next, after that, later*) to link paragraphs together

◆ use an impersonal style (avoid saying 'I' or 'me').

Write the first 150 words of your article. Use a headline like this:

The Night the Titanic Sank: Memories of a Survivor

Use a topic sentence for the opening paragraph (a sentence that summarizes the whole story – *who?, when?, where?*).

Finally, write a brief paragraph comparing your version with Millvina Dean's article.

◆ How different are they?

◆ How might they appeal to different audiences?

◆ What problems did you encounter in your rewriting?

Personal recounts
My First Day at School

Learning objectives

With these extracts we look at a variety of brief personal recounts, presented informally. You will study these objectives:

- Word level: develop your use of link words and phrases

- Sentence level: develop your understanding and use of subordinate clauses; become more skilful in managing tenses; improve your paragraphing skills

- Reading: extract information from texts; improve your note-making skills; develop your active reading strategies; identify the main ideas in a text

- Writing: explore different formats for planning; organize texts appropriately; use a range of presentation styles; improve your descriptive writing

- Speaking and listening: compare spoken recounts with written narratives; ask and answer questions well

---

Introduction

This section contains four short texts in which different people describe their first day at school. The extracts were first published in a newspaper article called 'My First Day at School'. Use them to develop your note-taking skills, and to explore the way writers use structure and details to bring their recounts alive. When you have finished, you will have a chance to write your own recount.

My First Day at School

The traumas and joys of starting school, as told to **Pamela Coleman**.

ESTHER RANTZEN, Chairman, ChildLine

I was two-and-three-quarters when I started school and it was a traumatic time. I did not want to go and on the first day sat very gloomily on the steps outside the house. My mother took me. I didn't scream and kick, I was just terribly miserable.

I know everybody is hugely in favour of pre-school play groups and nursery schools, but I remember thinking that making things out of egg boxes was pointless. I sent my own children to nursery school at three-and-a-half and I think that is a better age to start.

For the first three or four weeks at school I painted nothing but black pictures, which reflected how I felt at the time, and it was regarded as quite a breakthrough when I put my first dab of colour on the paper. Later on, however, I was one of those children who was very happy at school.

GLENYS KINNOCK, MEP for Wales

My grandmother lived next door to the national school in Holyhead in Anglesey, and on my first day I went to her house to have a cup of tea before joining my brother who was already in the juniors. I wasn't nervous about starting school.

The reception class teacher, Miss Morgan Jones, was very large and very cuddly and very nice. This was in 1949 and there weren't a lot of sweets about and my eyes immediately fell on a big Kilner jar of dolly mixtures, which was sitting on the mantelpiece. There was a fire in the grate and the milk crate was on the hearth to keep the little bottles of milk warm and the room felt very welcoming. There was also a rocking horse and one of those tubular steel rockers in which two children sat, one at each end.

At the end of the day you got a sweetie if you'd been good, and most children were good in Miss Morgan Jones's eyes.

BRIAN KEENAN
Novelist and former Beirut hostage

When I was held hostage I tried to remember my childhood, but I could never get beyond the age of eight or nine. I remember my first day at secondary school because the school was about four miles from where I lived in one of the tiny back streets of Belfast and I took a bus to get there. It was the first time I'd travelled on a bus without my parents.

All the lads in the street who were also starting at the school were with me and although I knew their faces, I was aware there was something different about them. What was different, I suddenly realized, was that we were all wearing school uniforms.

Everyone was apprehensive about starting a new school and there was an incessant din on the bus of boys talking and shouting. The school colours were orange and black – the badge on the jacket, the turn-down tops of the socks, the tie, the piping along the grey v-neck sweater you had to wear – and that and the noise of the scene reminded me of the swarm of bees or wasps.

BENJAMIN ZEPHANIAH
Poet

My twin sister, Velda, and I started school together at St Matthias primary in Hockley, Birmingham, which doesn't exist any more. When the time came for Mum to leave us with the teacher, Velda started crying and she wouldn't stop. Eventually she was moved to another room because she was causing such a disturbance.

I thought school was fun. I remember making a little building with building blocks and being surprised that all we did was play, because Mum had said you went to school to learn.

Velda and I were the only two black kids in the school, which frightened me a bit. After a while, when we could still hear Velda crying in the distance in some far corner of the school, the children asked me if she was my sister and I totally disowned her.

It's really weird the way things ended up: she really liked school later on and I hated it. She did well and I was the one who rebelled and got expelled.

UNDERSTANDING THE TEXT

1 Make a set of notes which show clearly:

- ◆ the name of each speaker

- ◆ what the speaker is best known for

- ◆ two or three main points of what they remember about the first day at school.

Hints

- ● Organize your notes clearly on the page – leave lots of space.

- ● Use bullet points to keep points brief (remember that you don't need to use full sentences for bullet points).

- ● Use underlining to add emphasis to the names of the people.

2 Glenys Kinnock has vivid memories of a teacher. Summarize the information we learn about this teacher.

INTERPRETING THE TEXT

3 Which speaker do you think has the most positive memory of the first day at school? How can you tell?

4 Which speaker has the least positive memory? Again, how can you tell?

5 Which speaker's experience of school sounds most *different* from the kind of school you first attended? Think about activities you did at school and the teachers you have known. Do they remind you of the experiences described by the writers? Write a brief paragraph to explain your answer.

LANGUAGE AND STRUCTURE

1 Recounts are usually divided into paragraphs about different parts of the subject. They may use complex sentences with subordinate clauses, where information is packed together densely.

Choose either the Glenys Kinnock or the Benjamin Zephaniah text. Then:

a write a very brief summary of what each paragraph is about (ideally try to use just one word – e.g. 'teacher', 'classroom', 'sister')

b write a sentence saying why the paragraphs are in this order – would they make sense in a different one?

c choose one paragraph and say how its opening sentence helps prepare the reader for some new information

d choose a complex sentence and say whether it is easy to follow or not.

2 Choose either the Esther Rantzen or the Brian Keenan text and look at whether the writer uses the past tense, present tense or both. Write down which it is, then give a reason why the writer may have used tenses in this way.

WRITING ACTIVITY

Think back to a teacher who made an impact on you. It might be someone in primary school or more recently. Think about:

◆ how the teacher looked

◆ the classroom he or she taught you in

◆ his or her personality and teaching style

◆ why the teacher made such an impression on you.

In pairs, talk about the teachers you remember. Using the bullet points above, ask questions about your partner's teacher. You might be asked to report back to the class on this teacher.

Next, write a three-paragraph summary of your memories of your own teacher. Use the same format as the texts in this unit.

Remember to:

◆ use the first person

◆ use the past tense

◆ use vivid details to bring the memory to life

◆ link paragraphs together with connectives.

Extended writing

Earlier in this unit you wrote a description of a teacher who had made an impression on you. Now think back to your memories of first going to school. What can you remember of:

◆ the school

◆ your first classroom

◆ your first teacher?

Write a recount which tells readers about your memory of the first day.

Aim to:

◆ use the past tense

◆ structure your ideas chronologically

◆ use connectives to link ideas together

◆ use a personal tone (e.g. 'I … me')

◆ use detail to help the reader visualize the scene.

Your main aim should be to entertain your reader. Try to bring the memory to life as vividly as you can.

What are explanation texts?

Purpose and audience

Explanation texts aim to help us understand the world. They may explain how something works, or why things are the way they are. They are often aimed at readers who have a particular interest in the topic, or who know a little and wish to know more. It is therefore essential that these texts are very clearly written and presented.

Text level features

The layout of these texts is often designed to help them get their explanations across to the reader. This might mean the use of **question and answer** formats, or **short paragraphs**, **bullet points** and **checklists**. Ideas may be structured in a **step-by-step** way, so that readers build their understanding logically. The steps may even be **numbered** to make the sequence clear.

Sentence level features

These texts will usually be written in the **present tense** – explaining how things are now (except where they are explaining an event from history). They might use the **active voice** (e.g. 'The scientist then places the magnesium in the dish …') or the **passive voice**, where the person doing the action is less important than what is done (e.g. 'The magnesium is then placed in the dish …'). The last part of the text might be a **summary**.

Word level features

The writer might include **specialist language**, depending on a) the topic and b) the audience. A glossary may be included to help explain any technical terms. The writing will usually be **direct** and **impersonal**, with little description, so that the essential facts are as clear as possible.

Formal and informal writing
Mobile Phones

Learning objectives

This section presents two texts for you to compare. They both aim to explain the same type of information. These are the objectives you will be studying:

- Word level: develop your use of link words and phrases

- Sentence level: improve your paragraphing skills; vary the formality of your writing according to audience and context

- Reading: compare the way information is presented; evaluate sources of information; identify the main ideas in a text; explore the way media texts are tailored to their audience; explore the features of some non-fiction texts

- Writing: develop your drafting skills; organize texts appropriately; link ideas in a text logically

Introduction

In this unit you can compare two texts. Both aim to explain a similar topic – the risks to young people of using mobile phones. Text A is a leaflet produced by the Department for Health. Text B is a page from the Newsround website, aimed at a young audience.

Compare the way the two texts explain the information. When you have finished, you can write an explanation text of your own.

Text A

Mobile phones and health: Children and young people under 16

Mobile phones are very popular with young people and have obvious attractions for personal security and keeping in touch with others. Parents and young people should make their own informed choices about the use of mobile phones. The current balance of evidence does not show health problems caused by using mobile phones. However the research does show that using mobile phones affects brain activity. There are also significant gaps in our scientific knowledge. Because the head and nervous system are still developing into the teenage years, the expert group considered that if there are any unrecognised health risks from mobile phone use, then children and young people might be more vulnerable than adults.

The expert group has therefore recommended that in line with a precautionary approach, the widespread use of mobile phones by children (under the age of 16) should be discouraged for non-essential calls.

In the light of this recommendation the UK Chief Medical Officers strongly advise that where children and young people do use mobile phones, they should be encouraged to:

- use mobile phones for essential purposes only
- keep all calls short – talking for long periods prolongs exposure and should be discouraged.

The UK CMOs recommend that if parents want to avoid their children being subject to any possible risk that might be identified in the future, the way to do so is to exercise their choice not to let their children use mobile phones.

Text B

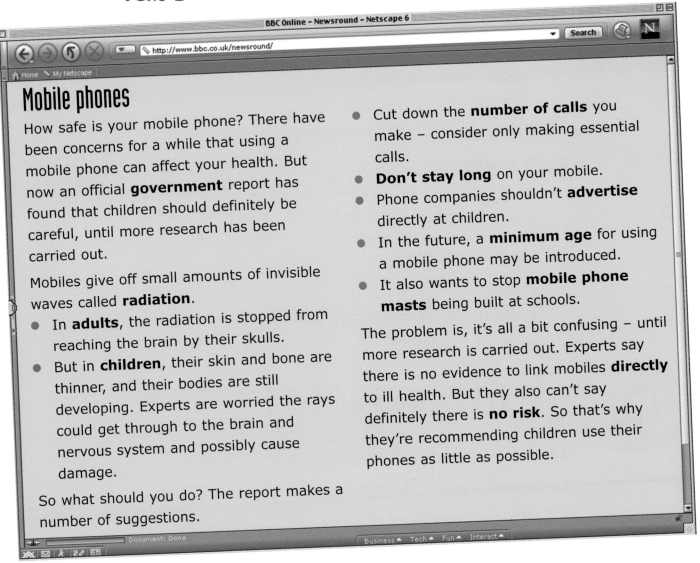

BBC Online - Newsround - Netscape 6

http://www.bbc.co.uk/newsround/

Home   My Netscape

Mobile phones

How safe is your mobile phone? There have been concerns for a while that using a mobile phone can affect your health. But now an official **government** report has found that children should definitely be careful, until more research has been carried out.

Mobiles give off small amounts of invisible waves called **radiation**.

- In **adults**, the radiation is stopped from reaching the brain by their skulls.
- But in **children**, their skin and bone are thinner, and their bodies are still developing. Experts are worried the rays could get through to the brain and nervous system and possibly cause damage.

So what should you do? The report makes a number of suggestions.

- Cut down the **number of calls** you make – consider only making essential calls.
- **Don't stay long** on your mobile.
- Phone companies shouldn't **advertise** directly at children.
- In the future, a **minimum age** for using a mobile phone may be introduced.
- It also wants to stop **mobile phone masts** being built at schools.

The problem is, it's all a bit confusing – until more research is carried out. Experts say there is no evidence to link mobiles **directly** to ill health. But they also can't say definitely there is **no risk**. So that's why they're recommending children use their phones as little as possible.

Document: Done

Business   Tech   Fun   Interact

UNDERSTANDING THE TEXT

Text A

1 What two reasons does the leaflet give for young people using mobile phones?

2 Does it state that mobile phones carry a health risk?

3 What are the findings of the expert group?

4 What are UK CMOs?

5 What advice does the leaflet give young people about using mobile phones?

Text B

6 What is the difference between adult and child skulls?

7 Does the website say that there are definite dangers in using mobile phones when you are young?

8 What is the advice about mobile phone masts at schools?

Both texts

9 When you were answering questions 1 to 8, which features of each text helped you to find the information you needed? Name one key feature of each text. You might mention something specific about:

- layout
- the way the information is structured
- the use of language.

INTERPRETING THE TEXT

10 In what ways is the information in the two texts similar?

11 In what ways does the information differ?

12 An explanation text should be carefully structured. Look more closely at the way these texts organize their information. How do the two writers structure their texts to make their explanations clear? You might look at:

◆ how the information is introduced at the beginning

◆ the sources that are given for the information

◆ how ideas are linked together by connectives

◆ layout features that help to present information.

LANGUAGE AND STRUCTURE

1 Look carefully at the two texts. Try to find a sentence from each text which states the same basic message. Write down these two sentences. Is there anything you notice about differences between the two sentences, such as:

◆ length

◆ complexity

◆ the kind of vocabulary the writer uses?

2 a What clues are there in the layout and structure that Text A is aimed at an older audience?

b How can you tell from the layout *and language* that Text B is aimed at a younger audience?

> ## Hint
> Look for any differences in:
> - the way the texts are organized
> - different types and lengths of sentences
> - different choices of words.

3 Looking more closely at Text B, can you say how you think information on websites is often presented differently?

4 Explanation texts sometimes include questions. The writer of Text B does this at the beginning of paragraphs 1 and 3. What is the purpose of these questions?

5 Look at this statement:

Text A uses scientific language and is more formal. Text B is less scientific and more informal.

Do you agree or disagree? Write down your answer giving an example from each text to support it.

WRITING ACTIVITY

Explanation texts aim to place their ideas in the order that will best help the reader to follow them. This means that sentences are often linked by connectives such as *because, next, another* or *so*. These words show how one sentence links to the next.

Take the list of facts on the next page. The sentences are presented in the wrong order. If you were using this information to create a fact sheet about Queen Elizabeth I, which order would you use? How would you link ideas using connectives? Present the information as a piece of continuous text for young readers.

Think about:

◆ how you will organize this information – dividing it into general points and examples

◆ how you will link the ideas together using connectives like *so* and *although*.

1. She was Queen of England from 1558 to 1603.

2. Elizabeth I was born in 1533.

3. She died in 1603.

4. At this time, England was in conflict with Spain.

5. Elizabeth I resisted getting married.

6. This was a period when explorers from Europe were sailing to discover new parts of the world.

7. New lands were claimed and new foodstuffs were brought back home.

8. Many people tried to arrange courtships for her.

9. The Spanish Armada was defeated by the English fleet in 1588.

10. It was a time of high adventure and excitement.

11. Courtiers included the Earl of Essex, the Earl of Leicester and Sir Walter Raleigh.

12. The war with Spain continued throughout her reign.

In pairs or groups, discuss how you approached this task and any problems you encountered.

Extended writing

Choose a topic you have been studying in a different subject – for example, something from Science, History or PSHE. Imagine your English teacher knows nothing about this topic. Your job is to explain it to her or him as clearly as possible on one side of A4.

Design a website or factsheet about the topic. Remember that you are being asked to *explain* a process or an event. Your text should answer a specific question, such as 'Why do trees need sunlight?' or 'Why are cigarettes so dangerous?'

Your teacher will then give you feedback on how clear your explanation was.

Think about:

◆ how you will organize your text

◆ how you will use layout features to make your explanation clearer

◆ how technical the information will be

◆ how formal your vocabulary and sentence types will be

◆ what tone you will use to address the reader.

What are instruction texts?

Purpose and audience

Instructions show the reader how to do something, usually in a sequence of steps. The level of detail in instructions will depend on how much the reader already knows. A 'Beginner's Guide to the Internet' may contain more general information than a specialist guide, such as 'Programming in HTML'.

Text level features

The **layout** will often be carefully designed to help the reader follow instructions – clarity will be essential. **Diagrams** may also be used to show how to do something. The text will be structured in a **logical order** and, to make it even clearer, points may be **numbered** in sequence. The writer might also add reassuring comments, or tips, to help the reader: 'Three quick steps to a delicious pudding …', 'If this seems time-consuming, don't worry – it will be worth it.'

Sentence level features

Sentences will often be **imperatives** (commands), with the verb near the beginning:

First **take** an egg. **Boil** it.

Sentences will often address the reader **directly**: 'If you need to check this …' They will often be **short**, so that they are simple to follow, and will use **connectives** to link ideas together, such as next, then, now.

Word level features

Vocabulary will often be **plain** and straightforward, except where the intended reader is already an expert in the topic. There will be little use of adjectives, adverbs and imagery: the writer will be aiming at clear instructional writing rather than using too much descriptive detail.

Giving informal instructions
Telepathic Powers

Learning objectives

With this extract we examine a straightforward set of instructions. These are the objectives you will be studying:

- Sentence level: explore the use of active and passive voice; sequence paragraphs appropriately; vary the formality of your writing according to audience and context; investigate the differences between speech and writing

- Reading: locate information in texts; develop your active reading strategies; identify the main ideas in a text; explore the features of some non-fiction texts

- Writing: organize texts appropriately; present information effectively; write instructions and directions

- Speaking and listening: give clear answers; give successful instructions and explanations; develop your knowledge of different types of spoken texts

Introduction

Instructional texts show people how to do things. This text is from a book of magic tricks. It aims to teach a young audience how to do a trick involving 'telepathic powers'. When you have finished studying it, try writing your own instructions. Before you read the text, look at the questions in 'Understanding the text'.

Telepathic Powers

Effect This is an ideal trick to perform at a party where there are lots of people.

Ask one of your friends to leave the room for a few moments. While he or she is out spread a number of cards around on the floor, face up. Now ask a second friend to point to one of the cards.

Explain that you are going to ask the first friend to return to the room and then you'll point to several different cards. When you point to the card chosen by the second friend, the first friend will call out '*that's it!*'

Emphasise that you will not speak to them nor give any secret signals – it's all done by telepathy.

Method You do in fact have a secret signal. But try as they might, your friends won't be able to discover it!

When you spread the cards (about 15 or 20) on the floor you make sure there are two or three picture cards among them.

When your friend is out of the room arrange for one card to be selected by another friend. The friend outside the room is now asked to return and you point to various cards.

The secret signal is that when you point to a picture card your friend knows that the *next* card will be the one selected by someone in the room.

If a picture card has been chosen as the selected card you simply point to one of the other picture cards first. Your friend will then know that the next card will be the selected one.

Presentation Explain that you and your friend have been experimenting with telepathy and want to demonstrate your amazing powers!

Variation This trick can also be performed with the cards face down. You will need a pack of cards with multicoloured backs. If there is black amongst the colours, all you do is point to other colours until you want to cue your confederate. You then point to the black area on the back and the next card will be the selected card.

You can also point to the top left hand corner until you cue your friend. The signal is that you point to the top right hand corner of a card and the next one is the selected card.

UNDERSTANDING THE TEXT

Before reading

1 Think about your own ability to give instructions. How clear and precise are you? If you were teaching someone to do a card trick, or to tie a school tie, how would you organize the instructions?

2 How would you change your instructions if the audience were older or younger?

3 If the audience already knew quite a bit about the topic, would that change the way you gave instructions?

4 Make some predictions about the text from the magic tricks book. It is aimed at a young audience, probably aged between 9 and 14. How do you predict it will address the audience? Will it be chatty, friendly, formal, impersonal? Will it address the reader as 'you'? Will it refer to the writer as 'I' and 'me'?

5 Look at the image used with the text. What does it suggest about when the book was written and who it is aimed at? Look at the way the children are sitting and how they are dressed. How would a modern image be different?

After reading

6 In a sentence, how does the trick work?

7 How does the 'variation' work?

8 In the picture, how can you tell who is doing the trick?

INTERPRETING THE TEXT

9 The writer has divided the text into short paragraphs, using some sub-headings. How could the writer have organized the information to make the instructions even clearer?

10 Look back at the predictions you made when you answered question 4. Write a brief review (two to three sentences) saying whether the writer's style is similar to what you predicted. For example, is the tone more or less chatty than you expected? What other differences or similarities were there?

LANGUAGE AND STRUCTURE

1 Instruction texts tend to use command sentences which begin with a verb, such as 'Ask one of your friends …'

   a Find another command sentence in this text.

   b Find a sentence which is a statement rather than a command.

2 The writer's style is sometimes formal. Look more closely at this paragraph:

If a picture card has been chosen as the selected card you simply point to one of the other picture cards first. Your friend will then know that the next card will be the selected one.

The first sentence starts by using the passive voice: 'If a picture card has been chosen ...'

a How could this sentence be written in the active voice?

> ## Hint
>
> ● You may want to use 'If your friend ...' as the beginning of the sentence.

b The final phrase 'the selected one' also sounds quite formal. Look at all of the second sentence and write it in a style that is more informal and friendly.

3 How would the instructions for this trick be different if you were *telling* a friend about the trick, rather than giving written instructions? How would you change:

◆ the overall structure

◆ the sentences

◆ the vocabulary

◆ the tone?

Would you address the audience differently?

Imagine you are speaking to a friend and telling her or him about the trick. Write down what you would say. Then write a brief paragraph describing the differences between your spoken version of the trick and the written version.

WRITING ACTIVITY

How could you use layout and language to make these instructions clearer and quicker for the reader to take in? You might use:

◆ headings, sub-headings and numbers

◆ diagrams and labels

◆ bullet points.

Produce your own version of the instructions on one side of A4, aiming for clear, simple vocabulary and sentence structures.

Extended writing

Working in pairs, give your partner instructions on how to do an everyday task – for example, tying a school tie, or tying up shoelaces. Give spoken instructions which your partner follows as you speak. Listen to the way you use language and how you know whether to add more information (e.g. 'no, not there – put it over the other side').

How would you give the information differently in a written text, where you could not react to the other person's actions?

Now try to write the 'Foolproof Guide' to tying a tie or shoelaces.

Write a set of instructions which you are certain will help even the most incompetent reader to get the process right.

You might:

◆ use step-by-step commands

◆ add friendly hints

◆ use diagrams and graphics to help make your instructions clearer.

Give your instructions to someone to test out. Ask for feedback. How well do your written instructions work? What could you have done to make them clearer?

What are descriptive texts?

Purpose and audience

Descriptive texts aim to give us detail. In a brochure, we might be given a description of a product. Both fiction and non-fiction writers will use descriptive writing to help us to visualize people or places. The level of description used will depend on the writer's aims. A short story may contain a brief but vivid description of a character; a film review may give a detailed description of the way a film is structured.

Text level features

These texts may begin with general **opening statements** (e.g. 'I remember my own schooldays') and then move into a series of descriptive sentences which add **detail** rather than new points. Nouns and verbs will often be modified by **adjectives** and **adverbs** (e.g. 'the *reddish* bricks', 'walking *painfully*').

Sentence level features

Descriptive texts may be in the **third person**, particularly in advertising and reviews; or they may use the **first person**, especially in autobiographical writing and some stories. The **tense** will vary too. Descriptions will often be in the present tense ('Ickworth Park is glorious in the spring'), except in fiction and autobiographical writing ('The school buildings looked large and threatening'). Sentences may be longer because they will use **modification** – adjectives and adverbs – to add detail.

Word level features

Vocabulary will be **precise** and **vivid**. There may be **imagery** (such as the use of similes and metaphors) in order to help the reader to visualize what is being described. The writer may use **technical words** in some contexts (a brochure about a new car, for example). **Connectives** such as *and, also, similarly* will be used to link ideas together.

Describing a place
Memories of Leeds

Learning objectives

This extract is an example of vivid description. You will be studying the following objectives:

- Sentence level: develop your understanding and use of subordinate clauses

- Reading: develop your active reading strategies; infer and deduce meanings; explore setting, character and mood; explore writers' language choices

- Writing: present information effectively; improve your descriptive writing

---

Introduction

Descriptive writing takes many forms. Here the journalist Keith Waterhouse thinks back to his childhood in Leeds and describes the excitement of wandering around the maze of old shops there. When you have finished studying it, you can try writing a vivid description of your own.

Glossary

polonies – spicy sausages

gastronomic – relating to food

aperture – small opening

clerestory – a row of high windows, as found in churches

hanker after – desire

Board Man – an inspector from the local Schools Board

Memories of Leeds

The Horse Meat Shop in the stew of tumbledown premises at the side of the Market was always a draw, principally because it took very little imagination to visualise the unappetising purplish joints and lumps of yellow fat in the window as horse, and partly because its frontage was painted in a vivid red, like blood; I liked to hear my mother tell me, as she often did, that it had to be painted this colour by law, to distinguish it from ordinary butchers' shops.

The herbalist's shop in Vicar Lane, with row upon row of little saucers containing powdered ginger, bee salve, prune and senna mixture, licorice root, cinnamon, dragon's blood (was it real dragon's blood?), was also good for a stare. So was the Murder Shop whose window display of scissors and kitchen knives I imagined in my confused way to be murder weapons. There was a secondhand bookshop at the bottom of Kirkgate where I could actually finger the old books in the nothing-over-sixpence trough outside, but it was to be some years before I would dare venture inside. Back to the modern: the Polyfoto studio on Boar Lane was a much talked about recent arrival to Leeds: the latest high-speed camera snapped twenty-four pictures of you and you selected those you wanted enlarged to the postcard or cabinet size from a specimen sheet. Examples of these multi-snap sheets were in the window and I would pause to count up in how many wasted exposures the subject was blinking.

The pork shops were always an attraction, and I would feast my eyes on their marble slabs of pies and pasties and polonies, not out of hunger but simply because these gastronomic displays were visually pleasing – particularly the bisected veal, ham and egg pies in Redman's in the County Arcade, which always left me puzzling how they got a whole hard-boiled egg into the middle of a meat pie. It was while I was figuring this out one day – they would cook an ordinary oblong pie, I reasoned, then scoop out an egg-shaped quantity of meat, then wedge the egg into the aperture, then seal the pie up again with some kind of edible glue – that I thought I spotted the Board Man keeping an eye on me from across the Arcade. It was not him at all, I saw at once, just someone waiting for his wife to come out of the corset shop; but it did set me wondering how I should explain things had the Board Man been following me and seen that while I had given barely a glance to the toy shop up the Arcade with its Meccano

suspension bridge in the window, here I was staring at pork pies and previous to that at the Horse Meat Shop and the Murder Shop, and then Montague Burton the Tailor of Taste (not only did I admire Burton's decorated clerestory glazing but I was beginning to hanker after a Burton's suit).

It was, as I could readily acknowledge in moments of insight, weird behaviour for a boy of eight or nine. I suppose I was a weird child all round.

UNDERSTANDING THE TEXT

1 What does Keith Waterhouse mean when he says that 'The Horse Meat Shop … was always a draw'?

2 What does he find particularly fascinating about that shop?

3 What was the Murder Shop? Why does he call it this?

4 How does his description of the herbalist's shop show that he is a child?

5 Why do you think Keith Waterhouse is anxious about the Board Man?

INTERPRETING THE TEXT

6 Which of these words best describes the way Keith Waterhouse presents himself in this extract?

curious   *fascinated*   *childish*   *nervous*   *optimistic*   *young*

Write a sentence explaining your choice.

7 How does the shopping area described feel different from town and city centres today? You might mention:

- ◆ the way the shops are organized
- ◆ what they sell
- ◆ their names
- ◆ what they look like.

LANGUAGE AND STRUCTURE

1 One way writers can create vivid description is by using lists of details within sentences, for example:

little saucers containing powdered ginger, bee salve, prune and senna mixture, licorice root …

a Write down another example of this 'list' technique in the text.

b What is the effect of this way of describing things?

2 Descriptive texts may also use words describing colour and texture. Write down some examples of Keith Waterhouse's words or phrases which use the senses of sight and touch.

3 The text uses mostly long, complex sentences, with many subordinate clauses. Why do you think Keith Waterhouse uses these rather than short, simple sentences?

> ## Hints
> - Think about the effect short sentences would have – how would the text feel different?
> - How do the long sentences, full of detail, help us to visualize the scene?

4 This is a personal piece of writing. In what ways does the writer use language that is personal – showing us the thoughts and feelings of a young child?

5 Writers can use imagery to bring their descriptions alive. Using your own words, write down the picture the following phrases create in your mind. The key words of each are highlighted. Does the image recall something you have seen or experienced yourself?

Image	The picture it creates
a Painted in a vivid red, like blood	
b The stew of tumbledown premises	
c The bisected veal, ham and egg pies	

6 How would Keith Waterhouse's writing seem without all the description? Write a one-paragraph factual version which focuses on what he does and where he goes, rather than on describing what he sees. Make it as bald and non-descriptive as you can.

Then write a sentence describing how you approached the task and what the final text is like.

WRITING ACTIVITY

Write a short, vivid description of a setting in your school – for example, a corridor at breaktime or the busy dining room. Focus on description, not plot or dialogue. Try to create a strong visual impression of what the place is like. You might:

◆ refer to sights, sounds and textures

◆ use imagery (similes and metaphors)

◆ use lists

◆ use long sentences, to create an impression of detailed description.

Extended writing

Working with a partner, talk about your memories of people or places. One of you (Student A) should choose a person or location in your school that you both know – for example, a teacher or classroom. Don't tell your partner who or where it is.

Student B is allowed 15 questions to try to identify the person or place. Student A can only answer 'yes' or 'no'. Start with general questions: 'Is this a room?' 'Is it used for teaching?' Gradually make your questions more and more specific.

Now think back to a place that meant a lot to you as a child. It might be the house you were brought up in, your first school, or a den you liked to play in.

Write a vivid description of the place. Like Keith Waterhouse, imagine yourself back in that location, describing the scene to help the reader to visualize it.

You might:

- start with a general sentence ('The smell of the school is my strongest memory …')
- write in long sentences, full of detail
- use adjectives and adverbs
- use similes and metaphors
- use words relating to the senses
- focus on pure description, rather than telling a story.

Assess Your Learning

Unit 1 Information texts

Work with a partner to review the work you produced for the writing activities on pages 17 and 21.

1 With your partner, read each piece of work carefully and look for evidence of the skills listed in the chart below. Copy the chart and record examples from your own work.

Formal writing skills	Examples	My progress
Use connectives to link ideas		○
Use mainly the third person		○
Use the present tense consistently throughout the text		○
Use examples to support points I have made		○
Use presentation to make the text look suitable for purpose and reader		○

2 Now assess your work. Decide with your partner which traffic light best matches your progress so far and colour it in the chart.

● I find this difficult to do.

◐ I'm doing quite well at this, but not all the time.

○ I'm doing well at this.

3 Look at the skills you have labelled yellow or red. Decide which two skills will be your targets next time you write a formal information text.

Unit 2 Recounts

1 a Look at the newspaper story you produced for the writing activity on pages 28 to 29. What have you learned about how to write this kind of text? Note down hints for:

- writing an effective opening

- structuring the story

- using connectives.

b Using your hints, give advice to a friend or small group about how to approach this kind of text.

2 a Work with a partner. Imagine you are the teacher and read the autobiographical writing your partner did for the extended writing task on page 34. Choose the best answer to these questions:

- Is a variety of sentences used?
  Yes   Sometimes   Not really

- Are the ideas linked together in an interesting way?
  Yes   Sometimes   Not really

- Is the reader's interest held throughout?
  Yes   Sometimes   Not really

b Then tell your partner what you think she or he should focus on next time you are asked to write an autobiographical text.

Unit 3 Explanation texts

1 Look at your work for the extended writing task on page 42 and annotate your writing to explain:

- how your information is introduced at the beginning

- how your information is linked together by connectives

- the reasons why you used particular layout features

- where you have used either technical or deliberately non-technical language

- where your sentence types and vocabulary are formal or informal.

2 Choose one of these points and write a sentence to explain what you would do differently next time.

Unit 4 Instruction texts

1 In this unit you have worked on your speaking skills. How did you do? Use the grid below to assess your progress, and give an example or some evidence for it.

Skills	Progress: 1 2 3	Example
Give clear and successful instructions and explanations		
Develop your knowledge of different spoken text types (e.g. telling someone about the magic trick, rather than giving instructions)		

Key to progress: 1 = not yet achieved   2 = achieved but not consistently
3 = consistently achieved

2 Here are some ways you could further improve your spoken instructions and explanations. Choose one of these suggestions, or develop an idea of your own, to help you improve your speaking.

- ◆ Give information in the right order to help the listener.
- ◆ Make logical links between ideas to make the sequence clear to the listener.
- ◆ Choose words precisely to make the meaning clear.
- ◆ Change what you are saying to respond to the reactions of the listener.

3 In which other subjects might you be able to practise these skills?

Unit 5 Descriptive texts

In this unit you have explored a descriptive text and written your own description.

1 Look at the answers you gave in 'Language and structure' on pages 52 to 53. Using the success criteria in the box, decide how well you were able to:

- ◆ find examples in the text
- ◆ explain the effects the writer achieves
- ◆ give personal responses or opinions
- ◆ work out implied meanings in the text (infer).

> **Assess your success**
>
> ✓✓✓ I did this effectively
>
> ✓ I did this sometimes
>
> ✗ I didn't do this at all

2 With a partner, look at your description for the extended writing task on page 54. Using the success criteria in the box, decide how well you used each of the techniques below. Find examples in your description to support your assessment.

- ◆ I referred to sights, sounds and textures.
- ◆ I used imagery (similes and metaphors).
- ◆ I used lists.
- ◆ I used long sentences.

3 What steps do you need to take next to improve your descriptive writing?

Persuade and analyse

Persuade and Analyse

Getting started
Unit 6 Persuasive writing

You have been asked to give feedback on ideas for a leaflet which aims to persuade more students to cycle or walk to school. Below is a list of possible opening sentences for the leaflet.

1 *Why don't you walk to school?*
2 *Experts recommend that we all need more physical exercise.*
3 *It's time to stop being lazy.*
4 *Have you considered walking to school?*
5 *Sack the chauffeur and get walking.*
6 *Use your journey to school to get fit.*

Working with a partner, decide whether you think each one is appropriate or inappropriate. Think about:

◆ the audience for the leaflet (students at your school)
◆ how clear the sentences are
◆ the tone the writer uses (is it friendly, humorous, serious, sarcastic, rude, formal, informal?).

Be ready to comment on each sentence, like this:

We think this sentence is appropriate/inappropriate because …

Unit 7 Discursive writing

Sometimes you have to put your own views to one side and present a balanced argument which gives the ideas for and against a topic.

Choose one of the topics below. Using the grid, think of arguments for and against.

Topics

a Students should be allowed to call teachers by their first names.

b Homework should be voluntary.

Topic:	
Arguments for	**Arguments against**

Unit 8 Advice

Look at these cartoons. All of them have something to do with giving advice.

1 Choose *two* of the cartoons and decide:

- **a** Who are the people in the cartoons?
- **b** What is happening?
- **c** Do the people in the cartoons already know anything about the subject?
- **d** What advice is being given?

2 Now choose *one* cartoon and write down some advice that the person in it might be giving. Then think about these questions:

- ◆ Which of the words you have written make it an advice text?

- ◆ How might you change the wording of the advice if the audience were older or younger?

Unit 9 Reviews and evaluations

1 Think of a TV soap opera or film you like and talk about it for 30 seconds to a partner. Your task is to evaluate the programme, saying what is successful and less successful about it. Talk about:

- ◆ the main storyline (in two or three sentences)
- ◆ the main characters
- ◆ the setting.

Try to use a range of adjectives, not just *good*, *bad*, or *boring*. Here are some suggestions:

lively	well constructed	sophisticated	fast paced	thoughtful
funny	well written	ambitious	disappointing	slow

Your partner should listen out for the different words you use in your evaluation.

2 Now think of the best ride you have been on at a theme park. Do the same thing again, describing the ride in detail in 30 seconds. In your last sentence, say why you thought it was so good (but without using *good*, *brilliant* or *amazing*).

Unit 6

What is persuasive writing?

Purpose and audience

Persuasive writing may express a point of view, or aim to change your opinions, or try to get you to buy something. It might be a letter or essay, an advertisement, a leaflet, or a television programme. Writers will often draw you into their world so that you can see things from their point of view. They will work on your feelings to try to get you to agree with them.

Text level features

The text may use **illustrations** to help persuade you – for example, in an advertisement a picture of a country scene may aim to suggest that a product is natural. It may use different **layout features** – such as font sizes – to make an impact. The writing may start with an **opening statement**, setting out the writer's views, and then go through them in more detail. The text will emphasize **key points**, and there will be **logical links** to guide the reader through the argument. The writer may use **humour** to get the reader on her or his side.

Sentence level features

The writer may use the **first person** (*I* and *me*) to express opinions, or may write using the **third person** (*she, he, they*) to create a more impersonal effect. Advertising will often be much more direct in its tone, using the **second person** and **imperatives** (commands): 'Phone us now for your free starter-pack'. Persuasive writing will usually be **active**, with short sentences for effect ('Don't you believe it!'). It will often use the **present tense**.

Word level features

Writers will choose powerful words to influence the reader, so you might expect **emotive** words such as *clash, fury, fiasco, disaster,* with writers sometimes overstating ideas (using **exaggerated language**) to make their point. In advertising, writers may use **word play** for effect, such as 'Beanz Meanz Heinz'.

Getting your point across
Rules Too Tight for Comfort

Learning objectives

This text puts forward a strongly argued point of view. These are the objectives you will be studying:

- Word level: develop your use of link words and phrases

- Sentence level: become more skilful in managing tenses; explore the use of active and passive voices; improve your paragraphing skills

- Reading: improve your note-making skills; identify the main ideas in a text; infer and deduce meanings; explore the features of non-fiction texts; explore writers' language choices; explore endings

- Writing: develop your drafting skills; organize texts appropriately; link ideas in a text logically; express a point of view; find different ways of backing up an argument

Introduction

This text is about having to wear school uniform. It was written by a 15-year-old student who expresses her opinions and tries to persuade us to agree with them. The article appeared in the *Times Educational Supplement*, a newspaper aimed at teachers. When you have studied this persuasive text, you can try writing one of your own.

Rules Too Tight for Comfort

Uniforms have a point but it's taken too far, says pupil Katharine Frazer-Barnes

THE IDEA OF SCHOOL UNIFORMS is to help create an atmosphere of equality between workmates. But are some schools getting carried away with what pupils can and can't wear?

When I moved up to secondary school, I was thrilled at the prospect of wearing a bright yellow shirt and a blazer which had the consistency of cardboard. I couldn't understand why some of the older students were so determined not to wear them; I was young, I was awe-struck, I was 11 years old.

So here I am, in Year 11, with my GCSEs looming, and I've turned into one of those typical 15-year-olds whom I couldn't understand when I started here.

Just the other day I was chastised for the 'amount of metal' I was wearing on my fingers, and a couple of weeks back a friend, who had dyed the tips of her hair red, was told to remove the colour or she'd get into trouble. I thought her hair looked wicked, but I wasn't going to argue with the head of year.

Back in my young, awe-struck days, I was under the impression that school uniform consisted of clothes alone: now I find that it dictates how many earrings you can wear, what colour your hair is, what footwear you can wear – even how your shirts should be worn.

Uniform has created many a fun game for us older students; one of the most popular is 'try to get into assembly without getting pulled over for incorrect uniform'. The idea is to avoid the watchful gaze of the prefects and staff while maintaining a sense of individual style. Some of us manage to pull it off, others end up in trouble. I have managed to avoid trouble so far.

I can see the point of uniform – in the clothes sense at least. Health and safety issues hold great importance in any school. A student who is working a fretsaw with massive clumps of metal hanging from her ears is a danger to herself.

And as staff keep telling us, it stops any feelings of inadequacy if you're not wearing the right clothes. But this is not a strong enough argument for making uniform compulsory; after all, there are so many ways to wear uniform, who says that you won't get ridiculed for the way you wear it?

Uniform is basically common sense. There is a place for it: if you're working machinery you don't want things to get caught. And if you're studying food technology, a grubby leather jacket is not hygienic.

But why are there rules on, for example, hair colour? As far as I know, (although the scientists may want to put me straight) dyeing your hair has absolutely no effect on your brain power.

And then there's uniform-induced bullying.

My younger school days were filled with fear at the prospect of an encounter with any of the pupils from neighbouring schools who when they saw anyone in a yellow shirt used to intimidate and in some, sadly not so rare, cases cause them harm. I was once pushed into the road by such bullies and for months afterwards hid inside a big pink duffel coat.

I suppose the experience and various incidents that have happened to friends have made me think quite hard about uniform. Consequently I've been strongly 'anti' since the middle of Year 8. Uniform has caused me far more problems than I thought any sort of code ever would. And in addition, whatever happened to freedom of expression?

And, if you want to talk to me about this article, I'll be the one with the orange hair, bejewelled fingers and unlaced Doc Martens. See you in detention.

UNDERSTANDING THE TEXT

1 What was the writer's attitude to uniform when she moved to secondary school?

2 How has her attitude changed now that she is in Year 11?

3 When did her attitude to uniform become strongly 'anti'?

4 What was the experience that helped to change her opinion?

5 What has she been in trouble at school for wearing?

6 What game do she and her friends play with their uniforms?

INTERPRETING THE TEXT

7 The text gives us a good idea of what the writer and her school are like.

  a What impression do you get of the writer? What sort of person is she? Support your answer with examples.

  b What impression do you get of the school she attends? Choose the word from those below that best describes it, and write a sentence to explain your choice:

    strict   fun   old-fashioned   formal   informal   traditional

8 Reread the article, making notes of its key points about school uniform. Based on your notes, make a list of the arguments for and against enforcing uniform rules.

LANGUAGE AND STRUCTURE

1 A well-structured text will use a different paragraph for each new idea. Look at the first five paragraphs of the article. Use the table to match up each paragraph with its topic.

Paragraph number (1–5)	Topic
	Looks back to when the writer was younger
	Gives an example of how she got into trouble
	Introduces the issue and raises a question about it
	Adds detail to what uniform actually means
	Describes how her attitude has now changed

2 a Now do the same for paragraphs 6, 7 and 8 – define what they are about.

b Does the writer's organization of her paragraphs help to get her arguments across? Say why or why not.

3 Persuasive texts often use the present tense. Look again at paragraphs 1 and 2. What tense is each paragraph written in? What is the reason for this?

4 Look at the way the writer signals that paragraph 2 is moving to a different period of her life: 'When I moved up …' This uses the past tense ('moved') and the discourse marker 'when'.

a Which words link paragraph 3 back to paragraph 2?

b Which words link paragraph 4 back to paragraph 3?

5 Most persuasive texts use the active voice to express ideas rather than the passive. Look at how one sentence from this text would be different in the passive voice:

Active	Passive
Uniform has created many a fun game for us older students …	Many a fun game has been created for us older students by uniform …

Why do you think it suits the writer to use the active voice throughout?

6 Like many writers of persuasive texts, Katharine Frazer-Barnes uses humour, including exaggerations such as these:

… *a blazer which had the* **consistency** *of* **cardboard**

… with **massive** clumps of **metal** hanging from her ears

a What is the name given to the sound effect used in the highlighted words?

b Do you think this type of imagery helps to make her arguments more persuasive? Why or why not?

7 How effective is the last paragraph of the article? How has the writer prepared her readers for this ending?

Hint

● Look for specific links between the ending of the article and what she writes in paragraphs 4, 5 and 6.

WRITING ACTIVITY

Imagine you are a teacher who has just read Katharine Frazer-Barnes's article in the newspaper. You disagree with her views on school uniform, and you want to write a letter to the newspaper to say so. Write the first two or three paragraphs of your reply.

◆ First, think about the points *in favour* of school uniform. Include evidence and examples from your own experience.

◆ Then think about the order in which you will organize them into paragraphs, and how you will make your letter persuasive (look at the techniques used in the article).

◆ Next, think about how you will start your letter.

You could begin with one of these opening sentences:

Dear Sir/Madam

I have just read Katharine Frazer-Barnes's opinion piece on school uniform. I disagree with her views for several reasons …

OR

So Katharine Frazer-Barnes isn't a fan of school uniform. Most pupils aren't. My view is …

Advertising
Asking for Support

Learning objectives

These two advertisements are aimed at persuading their readers to do different things. You will study the following objectives:

- Word level: develop your use of link words and phrases

- Sentence level: improve your paragraphing skills; increase the variety of sentences you use

- Reading: explore the way media texts are tailored to their audience; study the way print, sound and image help to create meaning; explore the features of non-fiction texts; explore writers' language choices

- Writing: develop your drafting skills; express a point of view

---

Introduction

Advertising is one of the most powerful forms of persuasive writing, and one we see around us all the time. Advertisements might be used to persuade us to buy a product (e.g. a certain brand of jeans), or to change our attitude (e.g. a political advertisement asking us to vote for a certain party), or to use certain services (e.g. join an organization).

Not all advertisements use text, of course. Some use images or sound effects.

This unit contains two advertisements. Both appeared in newspapers.

- One is persuading us to support an organization (Save the Children).

- One is promoting a product (the Barlow Knee Support).

When you have studied these advertisements, you will be able to devise one of your own.

Text A

In Huanta, Peru you don't talk to Ofsted about improving the school.

You talk to Eduardo.

Eduardo is not a schools inspector. Or a governor. Or even a teacher.

He is a pupil at one of the poorest schools in Peru. Until recently, he and most of his classmates felt the school was failing to give them the education they need. So they decided to do something about it.

With the support of Save the Children the pupils set up a school council to help improve standards. And Eduardo was voted mayor.

Now, under his leadership, the council is working closely with teachers to help bring the national curriculum to this desperately poor area. Little by little teaching standards are rising. And more children are getting the education they need to escape their poverty.

130 million children worldwide are missing out on a basic education. Helping them to improve their own schooling is just one of the ways in which Save the Children is tackling child poverty.

To find out how you can support our work during Save the Children Week, please call us on 020 7701 8916 or visit our website at www.savethechildren.org.uk

TAKE CHILDREN SERIOUSLY – HELP THEM CHANGE THE ODDS
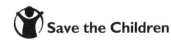

Text B

At last, here's instant relief for

Knee Pain

for men and women of all ages

DO YOUR knees ache? Do they hurt every time you take a step? Do you get twinges and shooting pains every time you twist them slightly? If this sounds familiar, you are not alone. Millions of people suffer from knee pain, often caused by a bad fall, old age, a torn or worn cartilage or simply an old accident or injury. All of these are a sign of your knees crying out for proper support. Support that really works.

FOR PEOPLE OF ALL AGES!

Nothing is more excruciating than knee pain, stiffness or strain! It doesn't matter whether it comes from a sports injury, a bad twist, a fall or simply from growing older, you'd give anything for pain free relief.

The remarkable Barlow Knee Support is guaranteed to bring you immediate relief or your money back. Imagine being able to walk, climb stairs, dance, jog and enjoy life again without pain.

The Barlow Knee Support was developed by veteran football coach "Cotton" Barlow when he found ordinary knee supports and elastic bandages just didn't do the job. He set out to add strength and stability directly to the joint where support and protection are needed most.

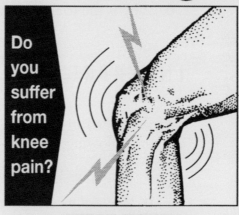

Do you suffer from knee pain?

THREE MONTH
NO-RISK TRIAL OFFER!

Order your Barlow Knee Support today and try it risk free for three whole months. We guarantee it will bring you instant relief from your knee pain – if it doesn't, we will refund you every penny of your purchase price without question.

AT LAST –
NEW RELIEF
FOR ALL WHO
SUFFER!

The Barlow Knee Support uses no metal, yet provides you with all the maximum lateral and cap support you need. This incredibly lightweight support absorbs shocks, prevents twisting and provides soothing warmth to injured or painful joints.

© 2001. The Bristol Group Ltd, 158 Moulsham Street, Chelmsford, CM2 0LD

FREEPHONE ORDERLINE
8.30am – 10.30pm – 7 days

0800 083 0941
(ORDERLINE *ONLY*)
If you require customer service, call 023 8066 5059

Quote Dept BKS86

RETURN TO: BRISTOL GROUP, DEPT BKS86, 36 STEPHENSON ROAD, TOTTON, SOUTHAMPTON, SO40 3YD
Please send me:
- ☐ 1 Knee Support @ £19.95 + £3 postage and handling
- ☐ 2 Knee Supports @ £37.90 + £3 postage and handling

<u>FOR CORRECT SIZE</u> Measure around the knee, one inch above the knee cap. My exact measurement is _____ inches.
- ☐ I enclose a cheque/PO for £_____ payable to Bristol Group
- ☐ Please charge my Visa/Master/Switch card number:

EXP. DATE_____ ISSUE NO_____ SIGNATURE_____

MR/MRS/MISS/MS _____

NAME _____

ADDRESS _____

_____

POST CODE _____

Delivery usually within one week but please allow up to 28 days. We hope to be able to bring you a variety of further interesting offers from reputable companies – if you prefer not to receive such offers, please tick this box ☐

UNDERSTANDING THE TEXT

Text A

1 Who is Eduardo?

2 Why did the children at the school want to do something?

3 How did Save the Children help in this?

Text B

4 Who invented the Barlow Knee Support?

5 What guarantee does the advertisement give?

6 Why is the trial offer at 'no risk'?

INTERPRETING THE TEXT

7 What do you think is the main aim of Text A? Choose from the following:

    a to help us learn about education in Peru

    b to make us recognize the work Save the Children is doing

    c to persuade us to send money to Save the Children

    d to persuade us to visit the Save the Children website

Write a sentence explaining your answer.

8 Advertisements always have their audience firmly in mind. Who do you think the different advertisements are aimed at? Look at the images as well as the text. Use the key words below to explain your answer for each product:

general audience   young people   older people

people with a shared interest/concern   mostly women   mostly men

You might write your responses like this:

Text A seems to be aimed at _____ because …

Text B seems to be aimed at _____ because …

9 Advertisements aim to persuade us to do something. Which text do you find most persuasive, and which least persuasive? Write a brief paragraph explaining your response.

LANGUAGE AND STRUCTURE

Text A

1 Persuasive texts often start with a strong opening statement. Look at the first paragraph of the main text:

Eduardo is not a schools inspector. Or a governor. Or even a teacher.

Most writers would present this as a continuous simple sentence, like this:

Eduardo is not a schools inspector, or a governor, or even a teacher.

What effect does the writer create by breaking it into three smaller units?

2 The headline of an advertisement is vitally important in attracting the reader's attention. In this headline, the writer uses the pronoun 'you'. Instead, he could have used a noun like 'people'. What effect does using the pronoun 'you' have?

3 Look at the structure of the text. For each paragraph:

a decide what the main function of the paragraph is

b write down any connectives or linking phrases which link the paragraph back to the one before it.

Paragraph	Does it aim to persuade, appeal to its audience, inform or entertain?	Connective/linking phrases (e.g. *and, then, gradually)*
1: 'Eduardo is …'		
2: 'He is a …'		
3: 'With the support …'		
4: 'Now, …'		
5: '130 million …'		
6: 'To find out …'		

c Now write a sentence describing what you notice about how the writer has organized the text overall.

Text B

4 Persuasive texts use a range of sentences, including statements, questions and commands.

   a Write down an example of each sentence function from the text.

   b Why do you think the writer uses questions at the beginning of the text?

   c Why do you think the writer uses a command near the end?

5 Advertisements usually aim to present a lot of information in a friendly way. The writer of Text B uses sub-headings throughout the text. What effect do these have?

6 Look at the structure of Text B. For each paragraph:

   a decide what the main function of the paragraph is

   b write down any connectives or linking phrases which link the paragraph back to the one before it.

Paragraph	Does it aim to persuade, appeal to its audience, inform or entertain?	Connectives/linking phrases (e.g. *and, then, gradually*)
1: 'Do your knees …'		
2: 'Nothing is …'		
3: 'The remarkable …'		
4: 'The Barlow …'		
5: 'The Barlow …'		
6: 'Order …'		

   c Now write a sentence describing what you notice about how the writer has organized the text overall.

7 Adverts often use exaggerated or emotive language to describe their product. Here are some adjectives and adverbs which Text B uses to describe the benefits of the Barlow Knee Support:

remarkable   immediate   incredibly   soothing

How do these words help the writer to persuade us that the product works well?

WRITING ACTIVITY

You might expect the advertisement for the Barlow Knee Support to be aimed more at people who participate in sport. How would you present the benefits of the product to an athletic, sporty audience?

- What image would you use?
- What headline would you use?
- How would you address the reader?

Sketch an outline to show what your advertisement would look like. Then write the first two or three paragraphs of the text.

You should:

- use the second person
- use questions
- use vocabulary relating to sport or athletics
- emphasize the reasons why the product may be useful to your target audience.

Then write a sentence describing the changes you have made to the original advertisement.

Extended writing

Choose one of the writing challenges in the panel below. Each of them is a difficult topic. Your job is to find a way of persuading your audience to agree with it. You can choose to write either an opinion piece (like the school uniform text) or an advertisement.

Persuasion topics

- Convince your audience of school students that it would be sensible to have fewer holidays and more school time.

- Convince your audience of footballers that football is a dangerous game that should be played only by professionals.

- Convince your audience that the use of computers should be limited to a small amount of time per day.

Starting points

- Decide what arguments you will use. Think of the arguments people would make against you, so that you can build answers to these into your writing.

- Think about the features of the text type you will use (opinion piece or advertisement).

- Plan your work, perhaps brainstorming ideas with others.

Think about:

- how you will organize your ideas. Will you put the most important points first?

- how you will use vocabulary that will convince your reader

- the sentences you will use – statements, questions or commands? Short or long? Simple, compound or complex?

- the evidence and examples you will use

- the links that will show how one idea follows on from another.

When you have written a few paragraphs, review them to see whether your style is really persuasive.

What is discursive writing?

Discursive writing aims to weigh up both sides of an argument. The writer usually gives her or his own opinion, but will also show what other people think.

Purpose and audience

Discursive writing is designed to present a balanced argument, often on a controversial issue. It often answers a question on a serious topic – for example, 'Is hunting cruel?' It might be an essay, a newspaper opinion piece or a magazine article.

Text level features

The title will often be a question or a controversial statement. The text will often be structured like this:

An **introduction** that announces the topic

Paragraphs showing different sides of the **argument**

A **conclusion** giving the writer's own view

The writer will often make a point (an **assertion**) and then back it up with supporting **evidence** or an **example**.

Sentence level features

The text will often use the **third person** (*he/she/they*) in order to keep the tone impersonal. It might use the **first person** (*I*) when giving the writer's own opinion. The writer will use **connectives** to show how arguments are related to each other – for example, *also, similarly, in contrast, on the other hand*. Many of the sentences will be **statements**, but the writer may use **rhetorical questions** for effect – for example, 'Is this true? We need to balance the evidence …'

Word level features

The writer may use **emotive words** and phrases to describe strong opinions. There may be words and phrases that are used to give **structure** to arguments – *in conclusion, similarly, despite this, therefore.*

Presenting a balanced argument

Pupils' Diets a 'Disgrace'

Learning objectives

This text is a website page that gives different opinions on the same topic. You will study the following objectives:

- Word level: develop your use of link words and phrases

- Sentence level: develop your understanding and use of subordinate clauses; use punctuation to clarify meaning; explore the use of active and passive voice; improve your paragraphing skills

- Reading: compare the way information is presented; identify the main ideas in a text; distinguish between the writer's views and others in the text; explore the way media texts are tailored to their audience

- Writing: explore different formats for planning; use writing to explore and develop your ideas; present information effectively; express a point of view

---

Introduction

News websites carry a range of information, and many people use the Internet as a main source of news. Website editors of the main news organizations therefore try to present a balanced picture – showing different viewpoints about a story.

When you have studied this discursive text, you can plan one of your own.

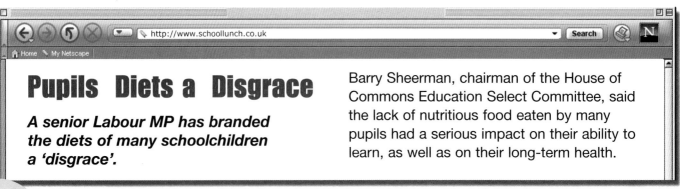

http://www.schoollunch.co.uk   Search

🏠 Home   My Netscape

Pupils Diets a Disgrace

A senior Labour MP has branded the diets of many schoolchildren a 'disgrace'.

Barry Sheerman, chairman of the House of Commons Education Select Committee, said the lack of nutritious food eaten by many pupils had a serious impact on their ability to learn, as well as on their long-term health.

He is calling on the government to spend more money on school meals to help improve the situation.

Speaking during a Commons debate on school meals, he said: 'If they want better food, they cannot flinch from the fact that better food does mean more expense, and that means a greater budget for schools for that service.'

Last year, the government published plans to improve standards of school meals.

Labour wants to introduce new minimum legal standards for all school meals in England.

The government's new standards include proposals to ban serving baked beans in primary schools more than once a week and chips more than three times a week.

School lunch: how healthy is your child's diet?

'Vague' plans

The guidelines – due to come into force from 2001 – also say fish must be an option at least once a week, red meat not more than three times a week, and that fresh fruit should be on offer at least twice a week.

But in its report on school meals, the committee criticised the plans as vague and unworkable.

It argued that banning individual food was the wrong approach, which would do little to draw children away from junk food.

It sided with health promoters such as the National Heart Forum (NHF) which said the plans would not stop children eating pizzas, for example, whenever chips are not on the menu.

The NHF also said the plans would not stop caterers cooking so-called healthy foods in an unhealthy way.

And it believes that rules about the quantity of nutrients that people should consume would be more effective than bans on particular foods.

Free meals

During Thursday's debate, Tory MP Nick St Aubyn acknowledged that chips, beans, sausages and burgers should not be removed from school menus altogether, as children's diets had to be attractive to them as well as nutritious.

But he said: 'There can be no doubt that well-fed children, those who've had something for breakfast before they come into class, those who have nutritious food during the day, are going to be more capable of concentration on their studies.'

A number of MPs called on the government to reinstate free school meals for all pupils, to help improve children's diets and school results.

UNDERSTANDING THE TEXT

1 Who is Barry Sheerman?

2 Why does he think pupils' diets are a disgrace?

3 What do government proposals recommend for:

    a baked beans

    b fish

    c red meat?

4 What is the NHF?

5 Nick St Aubyn says chips and burgers should not be totally removed from school menus. Why?

6 Who mentions a link between children's diets and their school work?

INTERPRETING THE TEXT

7 Discursive texts usually include a number of different opinions on their topic. This text gives various views on the subject of school meals. Use a grid like this one to show what different people say:

Who	Opinions
Barry Sheerman	
The Labour government	
National Heart Forum	
Nick St Aubyn	

LANGUAGE AND STRUCTURE

1 Look at the way this web page is organized.

   a What do you notice about the way the main text is divided into paragraphs?

> ## Hint
> ● Count the number of sentences in each paragraph.

   b Each sentence packs in a lot of information. Look at the one that follows the heading 'Free meals'. Where would you split this sentence, if you had to make it into two new sentences? Does putting it into a single sentence make Nick St Aubyn's argument easier or more difficult to follow?

2 Look at the headline. It could have said 'A Government committee criticizes school meals', but that doesn't sound like a headline. How does the web page headline aim to catch the reader's attention?

3 Look at the first sentence of the article. It is written using the active voice, starting with the subject: 'A senior Labour MP …'

   a How would it be written in the passive voice, starting with 'The diets of many schoolchildren …' as the subject?

   b Does this change the effect at all?

4 Discursive texts sometimes use rhetorical questions, as in the caption beneath the image. The structure is: phrase ('School lunch'), colon (:), question.

   a What is the function of the colon here?

   b Why do you think the writer uses a question?

   c What does the question tell you about the target audience?

5 In the first sentence of the article, the writer uses the verb 'branded'.

   a What other word might she or he have used?

   b Why do you think the verb 'branded' has been chosen?

6 Look at the sentence that follows the heading 'Vague plans'. It contains two dashes and two commas. Rewrite the sentence using another type of punctuation in place of the dashes.

> ## Hint
>
> ● The sentence already has commas, so try something else.

7 In this discursive text the writer discusses a number of different aspects of the topic in separate paragraphs, using connectives to link the paragraphs together. Find a paragraph where the writer begins with a connective showing that the following point will disagree with the previous one.

WRITING ACTIVITY

How would you design school lunch menus? What do you think the priority should be – good nutrition, or meals that students actually want?

If students are currently eating too many chips, burgers and beans, do you think that is a bad thing? Does it mean students need to be taught more about healthy eating? Should their eating habits be changed by teaching them about nutrition, or by changing what is on offer in school canteens?

Brainstorm the arguments for and against changing the menu in your school canteen, using a two-column grid like this:

Arguments for change	Arguments against change

Try to present a balanced set of arguments.

Now write a paragraph giving your own opinion, and the reasons for it.

Extended writing

How far do you think schools should *reflect* people's needs and behaviour?

How far do you think they should *shape* the way people behave? Look at this statement:

Schools have a duty to teach young people. This means that they should teach them to eat healthy food and keep fit. To do this they should serve only healthy food — no sweets, no pastries, no cans of soft drink — and they should place more emphasis on compulsory sport.

What is your first reaction? Do you agree or disagree?

Speaking and listening assignment

1 In a group, role-play a discussion in which each of you takes one of the parts below. Choose the mix of roles you would like to include in your discussion.

> **Some possible roles**
>
> ◆ Government minister who made the statement about the duty of schools
>
> ◆ Parent who believes children should be able to choose their own food
>
> ◆ PE teacher who would like to see more emphasis on health and fitness
>
> ◆ PE teacher who thinks that a strict policy on food and fitness could turn some pupils off healthy eating and sport
>
> ◆ Representative of the National Heart Forum, trying to promote healthy lifestyles
>
> ◆ Catering company manager — worried that the company might lose money if they are not allowed to serve popular foods

2 After your discussion, make a list of some of the different arguments that have been put forward in support of or against the proposal.

3 Describe the ways that the best speakers got their arguments across – for example, did they use jokes, or did they try to scare you into agreeing with them? Did they give convincing evidence to back up their arguments?

Essay assignment

Plan a discursive essay exploring the issue of school meals. Use this framework:

- Start with an introduction about the statement on page 83 on the duty of schools – describe who might have made it, and why.

- Give different points of view in separate paragraphs.

- Give your own opinion in the closing paragraph.

Remember to use the following features of discursive writing:

- Use the third person when writing about the topic and about other people's opinions. Then use the first person if you wish, to express your own view.

- Aim to support the different viewpoints with appropriate evidence, such as quotations or statistics.

- Use connectives to give structure to the different arguments (e.g. *also, in contrast, in spite of this*).

What are advice texts?

Purpose and audience

Advice texts aim to give us information which helps us. This means that, often, they are also persuasive texts – they aim to change our attitudes or behaviour. Often they will be addressed to a particular audience – for example, female or male readers of a magazine, or people with a special interest who are looking for advice on a topic (e.g. 'Increasing the Memory in Your PC'). Advice texts will sometimes share many of the features of instructions.

Text level features

The text may be organized around **questions** ('How can I best train my dog?') and it may be **illustrated** with photographs and diagrams to help give clear advice. Often it will address the reader using the **second person** ('You should start by making a list of everything that is worrying you'). Because the writer wants the reader to feel relaxed and confident about the advice, he or she will often use an **informal tone**.

Sentence level features

To make the text more informal the writer may use a **range of sentences**, including compound sentences (sentences joined by *and, or* or *but*). These can feel more relaxed, as if the writer is chatting to the reader. Sentence functions are likely to include **statements**, **questions** and **commands**.

Word level features

The writer will use some **description**, where it helps the reader. In general the vocabulary will be **simple** and straightforward, except where the advice is about a technical topic, in which case **technical terms** may be used. This will depend on the audience for the advice – the writer will want to use words that the reader will be familiar with, so that the advice seems reassuring and reliable.

Giving informal advice
Let's Get Physical!

Introduction

Newspapers and magazines often contain advice pages. This feature article is taken from a newspaper aimed at young readers. It is called the *Indy* and it was published by the *Independent* newspaper. This feature gives readers advice on spotting the 'secret signs' of body language. When you have studied it, you can try writing an advice page yourself.

Let's Get Physical!

You may be saying one thing, but your body will be saying another. **Louise Osmond** *and* **Phil Cool** *on the grammar of body language*

IMAGINE THE scene: you are at a party, you are attracted to someone, you want to make a move but you are afraid of being rejected. Does this sound familiar? Well, forget the sickly smile and sweaty palms. Body watching is your answer.

As a rule, people concentrate so hard on what they're saying that they forget that their movements, gestures and expressions are telling a story of their own. Body language can tell you what mood someone's in, what they're afraid of and just how interested in you they are.

Albert Mehrabian, author of *Silent Messages*, suggests that we can understand more about a person if we listen to their body language than we can if we listen to their voice.

Here is a basic body language survival kit. But remember, it's important not to read body gestures in isolation. Look for a collection of gestures; a combination of body signs that will add up to give you a general impression of your subject.

Seeing eye to eye:

THE FIRST and most crucial rule is to watch people's eyes. Eyes give out the most accurate and revealing of all the body's signals.

The pupils of the eyes dilate according to mood. They expand to up to four times their normal size when you're excited and reduce to tiny black dots when you're angry.

If you sense someone might be lying, watch their eyes. People who are lying will make eye contact for less than a third of the normal time (which is sixty or seventy per cent) and will look down or away from you as they speak.

Staring:

WHEN SOMEONE gazes intensely into your eyes it means one of two things:

Either he/she finds you very interesting or appealing, in which case their pupils will be big and fruity. Good news. Or else he/she is hostile to you and may be issuing a silent challenge. In this case the pupils will be constricted. Beware.

Arms and legs:

WATCH WHAT people do with their arms and legs. You will often find that someone with one or both arms folded across their body is in a nervous or negative mood, even if they are not conscious of it.

People disguise the building of arm barriers in any number of ways – pretending to wind up a watch, for example, or adjusting a bracelet, or simply fiddling with a sleeve.

Legs:

THIS IS a useful one to know at parties. Legs can tell you a lot about someone, particularly when their owner is standing up.

People often stand in groups at parties. If a member of the group has their legs and arms crossed, they are probably standing with strangers and wishing they could go home.

A person standing among friends looks very different. Their arms are relaxed and their palms are open. The open palms say: 'I've got nothing to hide, take from me what you want.' They are a sign of honesty.

Relaxed people lean on one foot and point the other towards anyone in the group they like or are attracted to.

Sitting down:

CROSSED LEGS should be read with care. Girls are taught from an early age that it is more 'lady-like' to sit down with crossed legs, and this can confuse things.

Luckily, the direction of the upper leg gives some clue to the person's mood. If the upper knee is pointing away from you it probably means something negative. If, however, the knee is pointing towards you, you may be on to a good thing. It could be a sign of positive interest.

Imitation:

COPYING SOMEONE'S gestures during a conversation is a sign of interest, agreement, or even affection. It's a sub-conscious instinct.

The sociologist Schleflen found that strangers often carefully avoid holding the same positions. But if they start to hit it off together, they will begin to perform a little pageant, tilting their heads at each other and crossing and uncrossing their legs in happy unison.

Deliberately mirroring someone can be a good way of putting them at their ease.

UNDERSTANDING THE TEXT

1 According to the first two paragraphs, what can body language tell you about a person?

2 Why is watching someone's eyes the most important rule?

3 What might it mean if someone imitates your body language?

INTERPRETING THE TEXT

4 Look more closely at the first paragraph. How does the writer try to hook the reader's interest in the topic?

5 Advice texts are often illustrated. What does the photograph used here add to the article overall? Does it:

   a help the reader to understand the article

   b make the article more serious

   c make the article less serious

   d demonstrate some specific examples?

Choose the statement you most agree with and write a sentence or two explaining your choice.

6 Which parts of the body language advice do you find convincing? Are there parts you do not agree with? Write a brief paragraph giving your response to the text, and saying how valuable you think its advice is.

7 Advice texts can use a lot of description to help the reader. Reread the text, and concentrate on visualizing the body language it is describing as you read. Does this technique help you to remember the main points of the article? After reading, write down as many points as you can remember.

8 How can you tell from the language used that the article is aimed at young people? Write down some examples to support your answer.

LANGUAGE AND STRUCTURE

1 The text uses sub-headings to organize the advice and information. The first four paragraphs do not have a sub-heading. How would you sum up what they are about? Try to find one word or phrase which could serve as a sub-heading for all of these paragraphs.

2 a Quickly scan the text to see how many different categories of body language it describes.

b How would this task have been different if the text did not have sub-headings?

3 Some advice texts use technical words that are suitable for their topic. This text says: 'The pupils of the eyes dilate'. Decide on another word or phrase that could be used instead of 'dilate'.

4 Advice texts often use command sentences, usually starting with imperative verbs, and directly addressing the reader: 'Imagine the scene …'

Look at paragraph 4, and write down the beginning of another command.

5 The writer uses a range of styles. Some are factual; some offer advice. Look at these sentences and, for each one, say whether it is fact (F) or advice (A). Then write down the main clue that helped you to decide:

a *If you sense someone might be lying, watch their eyes.*

b *A person standing among friends looks very different.*

c *Crossed legs should be read with care.*

d *Deliberately mirroring someone can be a good way of putting them at their ease.*

6 Advice texts are often written in an informal style. Look at this sentence:

Body language can tell you what mood someone's in, what they're afraid of and just how interested in you they are.

a In what ways does the writer's style seem quite informal?

b Rewrite the sentence in a more formal way, so that it feels less chatty.

7 Advice texts often support their main points with examples, to help the reader. Find a place in this text where a sentence giving general information is followed by a sentence offering an example.

WRITING ACTIVITY

Imagine you are writing an advice page for people who have not read this article. It will appear in a teenage magazine. Your piece is called 'How to Know if She/He Really Likes You'. Using some of the information from the *Independent* article, write down five main hints on the signs that someone should look for.

◆ Organize your points into a suitable order.

◆ Write your text as advice, rather than in a factual style.

◆ Remember to use imperative verbs ('look out for …').

◆ Remember to address your reader directly ('you …').

◆ Imagine your audience is the same sex as you (i.e. girls write to girls, and boys write to boys).

◆ Vary the structure of your sentences. You might want to use some conditional clauses: 'If he … then he probably …'

You might start like this:

Someone new just walked into your tutor group? How will you know what he/she thinks about you? Here's some advice …

First …

Next …

Extended writing

Choose a topic you know a lot about and write an advice sheet for a general reader.

Think of a title which begins 'How to …'

Some possible topics:

- How to win at … [name of a computer game]
- How to learn to skateboard
- How to improve your soccer skills
- How to write better stories

Consider your audience. They don't know as much as you do about the topic – but they are interested.

- Think about the vocabulary you will choose. Will you use technical words?
- Think about how you will address the reader.
- Think of ways to communicate your advice clearly – for example, by using sub-headings, diagrams, charts, a glossary of technical terms, or a separate 'hints panel'.

Start by planning the information you will use, including the 'How to …' heading. Then plan the layout of your advice sheet, and write the text (one side of A4 paper only).

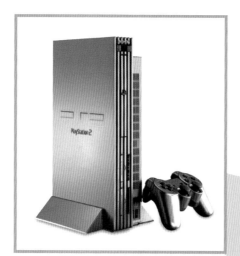

What is an evaluation?

Purpose and audience

Evaluations aim to discuss the strengths and weaknesses of something. It might be a play, a book we have read or a process – such as a technology project or science experiment. We sometimes write evaluations for our own use: they help us to reflect on what we did well and what we need to improve (e.g. setting personal targets in school reports). Other evaluations are used for assessment by others – for example, to show how well we have understood a process, such as a science experiment.

Text level features

The title may ask a **question**: 'What have I learned?' 'How well did the process work?' Writers might use **layout features** such as a table to list strengths and weaknesses, or bullet points.

Sentence level features

Evaluations will often be written in the **third person**. But even in an impersonal text, an evaluation section may be more personal, using the **first person** (I) to give a personal opinion. Evaluations will usually be written in the **past tense**. They will use **connectives** to organize points: *although, however, therefore, this shows that.* The best evaluations will avoid bland, meaningless comments such as 'It wasn't very good', and will give precise **detail**.

Word level features

The writer will use **technical terms**. She or he will include vocabulary that is related to **comment** – for example, 'I thought … I expected … I learned that …'

Writing an evaluation
Science Experiment

Introduction

In subjects such as Science and DT you will often be asked to evaluate a process. This usually forms the final part of an assignment. The example given here was written by Tom Fullam, a student in Suffolk. It is part of his report of a science experiment. The final section shows how he approached the evaluation. When you have read his work, you will be able to write your own version of his evaluation.

Glossary

radiation – *the sending out of heat or light, etc. in rays*

emit – *to send out, give off*

Science Experiment

Aim: To investigate the effect of different colours on the rate of cooling of water.

Introduction: We did a preliminary experiment involving only two colours, matt black and silver foil.

We carried out a preliminary experiment, where we measured the temperature change over 10 minutes in two test tubes of hot water (75°C) as they cooled. One was covered with foil, and one was covered with black paper.

The foil covered tube cooled by 18°C.
The black paper covered tube cooled by 21°C.

Dull black surfaces are the best absorbers of radiation. They reflect hardly any radiation at all.

Shiny silver surfaces are the worst absorbers of radiation. They reflect nearly all the radiation that strikes them.

Best absorbers

Worst absorbers

Best emitters

Worst emitters

Dull black surfaces are the best emitters of radiation.

Silvery surfaces are the worst emitters of radiation.

Hypothesis: I predict that the water in the test tube covered in black paper will cool the quickest. This is because the black outer surface will radiate the heat into the air in the room, while the surface inside the tube will absorb the heat well.

The silver foil covered test tube will cool the slowest, because its silvery surface will not absorb the heat radiation well. Also, because the outer surface is also silvery, the heat that does get absorbed will not be radiated effectively into the room.

The white paper covered tube is not as good at absorbing and radiating heat as the black paper, but it is better than the silver.

Apparatus:

4 test tubes	Test tube rack
Black paper	Goggles
Silver foil	Kettle (to supply the hot water)
White paper	Cotton wool (to use in absence of a rubber bung)
Timer	Thermometer

To ensure a fair test, the width and layers of the foil and paper must be as equal as possible. The test will last 15 minutes, to get a well-spread set of results, and the experiment will be repeated 3 times, for the same reasons.

Method:
- For safety, goggles will be worn.
- Cover a test tube with black paper, another tube with white paper, another with foil, and the last tube is left alone (as a control). Make sure only one layer of paper/foil is put on each appropriate test tube.
- Measure out freshly boiled water into 4 equal 35cm³ amounts.
- Put the test tubes into the test tube rack, and pour the 35cm³ measures of water into each tube.
- Put the thermometers into each tube, and let them rest on the bottom of the tube.
- Plug the hole in the top of the tubes with equal amounts of cotton wool.
- When the temperature has levelled out (after several seconds) start recording the temperatures (every minute, for 15 minutes, including the starting temperature at minute 0).
- Repeat the experiment 3 times to get an average.

Fair test: The following things will be done to make sure that the experiment is a fair test.
- The temperature on the thermometers must have settled before the timers are started, as there is a small amount of inaccuracy.
- The height of the thermometers will be the same, because convection currents may make the temperature different if the thermometer rests higher or lower.
- The test tubes will all be the same size, then they will have the same surface area. The surface area affects the cooling rate of the water.
- One layer of paper/foil will be used. If there are more layers wrapped around the tube, then they could trap unequal amounts of air (to form insulation).
- The kettle will be freshly boiled each time, to keep the starting temperatures the same.

Results:

Time in minutes	Black temp (°)	White temp (°)	Foil temp (°)	Control temp (°)
0	60	60	60	60
1	58	58	57	57
2	56	56	55	55
3	55	55	53	53
4	54	53	52	51
5	52	52	50	49
6	51	51	48	47
7	49	49	46	46
8	48	49	46	44
9	47	47	45	43
10	46	46	44	42
11	45	45	42	40
12	44	44	42	39
13	43	43	41	38
14	43	43	40	38
15	42	41	39	37

Conclusion: The results of the experiment seemed to indicate that matt black was the better colour, even though my prediction and various textbooks stated otherwise. The evidence of this being incorrect is also shown by the fact that there seemed to be no major differences between the temperatures the materials kept the water at, with only an average range of 5. However, since the control tube had the lowest temperature, this indicates that surfaces of differing radiating abilities all had a positive effect on the water temperature-cooling rate. Tin foil SHOULD have kept the highest temperature, but it appeared to be the second lowest.

Evaluation: Although I did not notice anything go drastically wrong with the experiment, there seemed to be an incorrect result to it, with the black paper seemingly better at retaining heat. Several factors could have made this possible. The cotton wool we used to bung the test tubes was varying in thickness, so the black paper could have had a thick wedge, while the silver foil could have had a thinner one, allowing more heat to escape. Also, the test tubes had the hot water added to them in the same order, so by the time it had reached the silver foil encased tube, it could have marginally cooled down, changing our results. Also, the black paper was thicker than the silver foil, so it could work as a better insulator. These factors made the experiment unfair. If I could repeat the experiment, I would use proper rubber bungs of equal density, and use four kettles (something that was not possible when we did the experiment). This would have made the information both more reliable and more accurate.

UNDERSTANDING THE TEXT

1 In your own words, describe what the experiment is designed to find out.

2 What did Tom Fullam predict would be the result?

3 What surprised him about the result?

4 Give one clue from the text that Tom has paid attention to safety issues.

5 Scan the text to find:

   a how many things were done to make sure the experiment was a fair test

   b the time in minutes that it took the 'control' test tube to cool to 49°.

INTERPRETING THE TEXT

6 What do you learn from the diagram Tom uses? Do you learn anything from the diagram and labels that is not mentioned in the text?

7 How can you tell that the text is aimed at a specialist audience – readers who already know something about science experiments?

Hints

- Look at the vocabulary Tom chooses.
- Look at the sub-headings he uses to organize his text.

8 What does his 'Evaluation' section show Tom has learned from the experiment?

9 Reread Tom's 'Hypothesis' section. Now complete the following sentences, comparing what he predicts about the different test tubes:

The test tube covered in … will cool most quickly.

The test tube covered in … will cool more slowly than this.

The test tube covered in … will cool most slowly of all.

LANGUAGE AND STRUCTURE

1 Evaluations use a range of layout features to help make the information clear, including sub-headings.

   a How do the sub-headings in this text help the reader?

   b Under his sub-headings, does Tom organize his paragraphs well, or are any of them too long or too short? Explain your answer.

2 In some places, the writer uses the present tense; in some he uses the past; and in others he uses the future tense.

Look at the sentences below. For each one say which tense Tom is using and why you think he does this.

Example	Tense	Reason
We did a preliminary experiment involving only two colours.		
The silver-foil covered test tube will cool the slowest.		
The white-paper covered tube is not as good at absorbing and radiating heat as the black paper, but it is better than the silver.		

3 a What tense would you expect the writer to use for an evaluation?

b Does Tom use this tense throughout his 'Evaluation' section? If not, why not?

4 Tom uses the passive voice in parts of his assignment. For each of the examples below, write down how they could be written in the active voice:

Passive version	Active version
For safety, goggles will be worn.	
The kettle will be freshly boiled each time.	
The test tubes had the hot water added to them.	

5 In his 'Conclusion' and 'Evaluation' sections, Tom uses a number of connectives to join his ideas together. Write down three connectives he uses.

6 Evaluations often use technical or specialist terms. Write down three examples of technical words that Tom uses. For each one, try to think of an everyday word that means something similar.

WRITING ACTIVITY

Tom Fullam's assignment is written in quite a formal style. His words would be very different if he was just chatting to a friend after doing the experiment.

His friend asks what he did last lesson, and Tom briefly describes the experiment. How would his use of language be different from the formal assignment? Write part of Tom's spoken account, using words and structures that we find in spoken language. You could start like this:

Friend: So what were you doing last lesson?

Tom: Well, we were doing an experiment to try and find out
        how …

Your account should include Tom's evaluation of whether
the experiment went well or badly, and why.

When you have finished, write a sentence describing the
main ways in which your spoken version differs from the
text written by Tom.

UNIT 9

Writing a review
Teenage Fiction

Learning objectives

These texts are book reviews – one taken from a website, the other from a newspaper. You will study the following objectives:

- Word level: explore words in their context

- Sentence level: identify the main point in a paragraph; increase the variety of sentences you use; become familiar with the conventions of different text types

- Reading: identify the main ideas in a text; infer and deduce meanings; explore the features of non-fiction texts

- Writing: present findings and express a personal view; write reflectively about a text

Introduction

Reviews appear in magazines and newspapers and on websites. They aim to evaluate the quality of different products – from new cars to plays and films, books, even the food in restaurants. A reviewer usually describes the features of the book, play or film he or she is reviewing, and then evaluates how successful it is.

Reviews share many of the features of evaluations (see page 93), but often use the first and second person to give personal views and to address the reader directly. They are often written in the present tense.

The following texts are two book reviews written in very different styles. Text A is from the website Bookheads, which collects and publishes reviews of teenage fiction. It was written by Mark Haddon, author of *The Curious Incident of the Dog in the Night-time*. Text B is an edited version of a newspaper review of recommended books for teenage readers, written by Amanda Craig for the *Independent*.

Look at the way the writers communicate their opinions, and how they use language and organization to make their point.

Text A

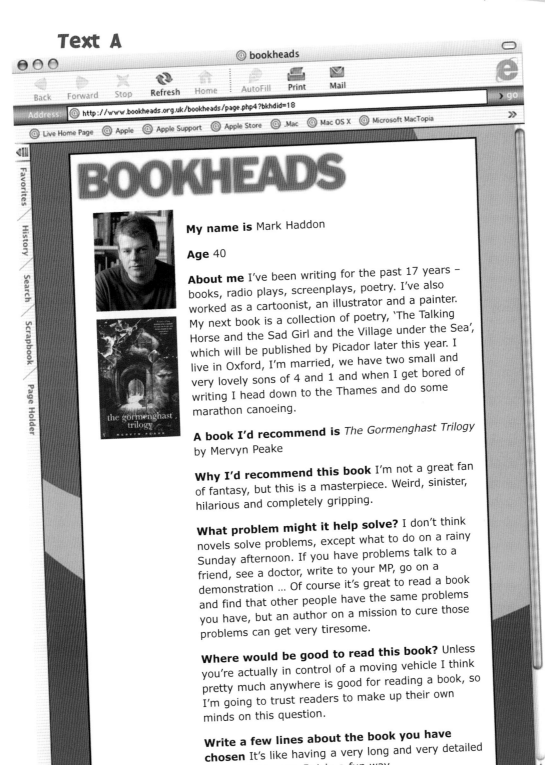

BOOKHEADS

My name is Mark Haddon

Age 40

About me I've been writing for the past 17 years – books, radio plays, screenplays, poetry. I've also worked as a cartoonist, an illustrator and a painter. My next book is a collection of poetry, 'The Talking Horse and the Sad Girl and the Village under the Sea', which will be published by Picador later this year. I live in Oxford, I'm married, we have two small and very lovely sons of 4 and 1 and when I get bored of writing I head down to the Thames and do some marathon canoeing.

A book I'd recommend is The Gormenghast Trilogy by Mervyn Peake

Why I'd recommend this book I'm not a great fan of fantasy, but this is a masterpiece. Weird, sinister, hilarious and completely gripping.

What problem might it help solve? I don't think novels solve problems, except what to do on a rainy Sunday afternoon. If you have problems talk to a friend, see a doctor, write to your MP, go on a demonstration … Of course it's great to read a book and find that other people have the same problems you have, but an author on a mission to cure those problems can get very tiresome.

Where would be good to read this book? Unless you're actually in control of a moving vehicle I think pretty much anywhere is good for reading a book, so I'm going to trust readers to make up their own minds on this question.

Write a few lines about the book you have chosen It's like having a very long and very detailed Gothic nightmare. But in a fun way.

Text B

Thrill to the manaxa
A choice of books for older readers

by Amanda Craig

When I was a child I spent my pocket money on books, not sweets. This wasn't virtue – I lived abroad, there was no TV, and children's books were rare. Being paperbacks, my own 5 purchases have mostly fallen to bits, but a handful remain family treasures. These were given me by a remarkable babysitter called Paddy Fraser to whom I've been grateful all 10 my life, not only for understanding what a great book is but for giving me hardbacks. Whenever I read a children's novel I ask: would this pass the Paddy test? Both JK Rowling and 15 Philip Pullman would, but not many others.

Marcus Sedgwick's *Floodland* was a successful, high-concept novel set in the future. His second, *Witch Hill* 20 (Dolphin £4.99), is more traditional, skilfully mixing past and present in the tale of Jamie's pursuit by a terrifying witch, and of the fire that caused a family tragedy. Sedgwick is 25 good at conveying isolation and fear, and his second novel will appeal to those with a taste for horror and the supernatural. The trouble is, his happy endings seem forced and 30 unconvincing.

At least his books do have endings. David Almond's *Secret Heart* (Hodder £10) takes the magic realism style that won deserved praise for *Skellig* 35 and *Kit Wilderness* to less productive extremes. Its hero, Joe Maloney, truants from school and dreams of tigers. His one friend, Stanny, wants to teach him how to kill, and a new 40 friend from the circus tells him about

the dreams of the past. Almond writes beautiful prose, but children will be as fed up as I was, because practically nothing happens.

Castaways of the Flying Dutchman (Viking £12.99) marks a big change from Brian Jacques's best-selling 'Redwall' books. The dumb Ned and his dog are stowaways on the fateful ship. The villainous crew are doomed to roam the world for ever, but Ben and Ned bring help to wherever it's needed – in this case, a 19th-century village at risk from ruthless developers. Stirring stuff, though the writing is rather flat.

Jacqueline Wilson's success is a bit of a mystery to me, though she deserves praise for tackling subjects like manic depression in *The Illustrated Mum*. Her latest, *The Cat Mummy* (Doubleday £10.99), is about Verity's relationship with her elderly cat, Mabel. When Mabel disappears, Verity, whose mother is dead, becomes obsessed with Ancient Egypt. It's all quite sweet, though as a story about bereavement and cats not a patch on Paul Gallico's *Jennie*.

William Nicholson wrote the script for *Gladiator*. His *The Wind Singer* (Mammoth £5.99) won a Smarties Gold Award last year, and its sequel, *Slaves of the Mastery* (£10.99), is even better. Gloriously cinematic and completely enthralling, it is about revenge, music, courage, fighting and family loyalty. A city is taken into slavery, and only one family, which develops its hereditary gift of prophecy and telepathy, fights back. Boys will thrill to the manaxa, a deadly but beautiful gladiatorial fighting style. Here are characters who care about each other, and whose hearts fill with passion, humour and the kind of rebelliousness that is the hallmark of a terrific new children's author.

Lastly, the good news is that Red Fox are republishing selected classics on their list (£4.99), including E Nesbit's glorious time-travel classic, *The House of Arden*, in September. Hurrah! It does amaze me the way children's publishers such as Penguin fail to treasure their backlists, though this is good news for Jane Nissen Books, whose entire list of reprinted children's classics is a joy to read. Next month Jane Nissen republishes Noel Streatfield's *Tennis Shoes* and Pauline Clarke's classic about the Brontë children's magical toy soldiers, *The Twelve and the Genii* (£6.99). One other noteworthy event is the reissue of Edward Eager's *Magic by the Lake* and *The Time Garden* by OUP (£4.99). I can't recommend these gentle, quirky adventures too highly.

UNDERSTANDING THE TEXT

Text A

1 What different jobs has Mark Haddon had, apart from writing?

2 At what age did he begin writing?

3 Which word does he use to show that he finds *The Gormenghast Trilogy* funny?

Text B

4 Philip Pullman was Amanda Craig's babysitter – true or false?

5 For what two reasons is she grateful to her babysitter?

6 What was the main reason why she had so few books at home?

INTERPRETING THE TEXT

Text A

7 Mark Haddon says: 'If you have problems talk to a friend, see a doctor …' Why does he say this when asked what problem a book might solve?

8 Find another example in which he answers a question in a quirky, funny way.

Text B

9 Using a spider diagram, write down some notes on what we learn about Amanda Craig from the article. Think about her background, her tastes in reading, and her opinions.

Both texts

10 Both writers have strong opinions. Write down a sentence from each text that demonstrates their strong views.

11 Which writer seems to have the stronger opinions?

12 Which novel does Amanda Craig, the writer of Text B, seem to like most? Which does she like least?

LANGUAGE AND STRUCTURE

1 Text A uses questions and statements to structure the text. Think of three other questions or statements that could be used to make the review more detailed.

2 Text B starts with an introduction. How are the later paragraphs organized? What is the structure of the writing?

3 Here is a theory about how the writer of Text B structures her review:

   Each paragraph (apart from the first one) is organized in this way:

   ◆ *First she gives a flavour of the novel she is reviewing (description).*

   ◆ *Then she says what she thinks about it (evaluation).*

   Choose three paragraphs from Text B. Does each one use this structure? Present your answer like this:

Paragraph number	Does it use the description/evaluation structure?
	Yes/No
	Yes/No
	Yes/No

4 Which words does Mark Haddon use in Text A to show his enthusiasm for the book?

5 Which words in Text B show the writer's enthusiasm?

6 **a** Explain what you understand from this answer in Text A:

   It's like having a very long and very detailed Gothic nightmare. But in a fun way.

   b Why do you think the writer uses two sentences in this answer rather than one?

7 Find some examples of words in Text B that the writer uses to link her ideas together (e.g. *lastly*, *also*).

8 The writer of Text B, Amanda Craig, uses some technical language to express her opinions. Look at the examples below. Think of another way of expressing each idea.

Amanda Craig's language	The same idea in simpler language
his happy endings seem forced and unconvincing (lines 30–31)	
the writing is rather flat (line 57)	
completely enthralling (line 77)	
a joy to read (line 101)	

9 Answer the questions below. Support your point of view – for example, with an explanation or quotation from the text.

Which writer's style is:

a easier to follow

b more informative

c more formal

d more interesting

e more detailed?

10 Look more closely at the way Amanda Craig expresses her opinions. Find an example of a sentence that is purely factual. Then find an example of a sentence that is an opinion. What do you think is the main difference between the two sentences?

WRITING ACTIVITY

1 Imagine you are asked to review a book for the Bookheads website. Choose one of the books Amanda Craig writes about in Text B and try to write about it in the style used in Text A, using the same sub-headings.

Think about:

◆ your choice of vocabulary

◆ how you can use simpler sentences.

2 Take your own favourite book and either present your ideas in the format used in Text A, or write a one-paragraph review, as in Text B. Whichever format you choose, make your review informative, entertaining and fun to read.

Unit 9

Extended writing

Write a review of something you have recently seen, read or experienced.

You might choose:

- ◆ a book
- ◆ a magazine
- ◆ a CD
- ◆ a play, film or TV programme
- ◆ a meal (including one you ate at school)
- ◆ a computer game.

You are writing for a general audience, and your aims are:

- ◆ to give detailed information about your subject and what it involves (you might mention characters, music, animations, language, pace, structure … as appropriate)
- ◆ to tell them how good it is.

Think about the structure of your review.

- ◆ You probably want to start with a general statement about your subject (e.g. 'This is the latest release …') or information about who it is by.
- ◆ Then you might use a number of paragraphs to focus on different aspects (features) of your subject (e.g. for a book review you would want to discuss characters, plot, setting and language).
- ◆ Finally, you will want to give an evaluation of your subject, using adjectives that show your opinion (e.g. *successful, fast paced, boring, tense, enjoyable, well crafted, unoriginal, predictable*)

Remember to:

- ◆ find ways of keeping the reader interested (e.g. vary your sentences)
- ◆ avoid saying 'I' too much
- ◆ use the present tense, mostly
- ◆ give specific examples, including quotations, where possible.

Unit 6 Persuasive writing

Look back at a piece of writing you have produced in this unit.
Complete a learning diary for it. You can use the sentence starters
below to help you.

What I did

To plan the content of the writing I …
To organize my ideas I …
In the first paragraph I tried to …
While I was writing I also …
In the final paragraph I decided to …

What I have learned

I have learned how to …
I have improved at …
I have made progress in my ability to …

My targets

Next time, I will try to …
To achieve this, I will …

Unit 7 Discursive writing

Review your contribution in the speaking and listening assignment
on pages 83 to 84. You could also ask a friend in your group for
his or her comments on the role you played. Complete a chart like
the one below. You can use the key words listed on page 112 to
help you.

Date	My role was …	My contribution was good because …	My friend's comment was …	I could improve my speaking and listening by …
	This meant I had to speak …			

Key words:

- expressed my point of view
- asked questions to develop ideas
- used supporting evidence
- asked rhetorical questions
- used connectives
- spoken clearly and confidently
- took an active part in the discussion
- listened carefully to other speakers
- adjusted my point of view after listening to others

Unit 8 Advice

1 a In the extended writing task on page 92, you had a chance to show your command of subject vocabulary on a topic you know something about. Look back over your work and highlight some of the subject-specific words you used.

b Now choose another topic and write a list of five words which show that you are an expert in this topic.

c Choose one of the words on your list. If someone knew nothing about the topic, would you:

- still use the technical word?
- use a more general word instead? If so, which word would you choose?
- use the technical word but explain it as well? If so, how would you explain it?

2 a Here are some of the things writers need to think about when writing advice:

- Hook the reader's interest.
- Use description to help the reader.
- Choose a formal or informal style appropriately.
- Support main points with examples.
- Write the information as advice rather than factual statements.

◆ Use a range of sentence structures, including the conditional (e.g. 'If she … then she will …').

◆ Address the reader directly ('you').

◆ Choose between technical words and everyday explanations of technical details.

◆ Use commands.

◆ Use presentation features to make the advice clear.

Choose one thing from the list that you did well. Find the evidence in your work and write a comment explaining the effect on the reader.

b Choose one thing that you think you need to develop. At the end of your work, write some advice for yourself on how to do it.

Unit 9 Reviews and evaluations

This activity helps you to assess the reading activities you have completed in this unit.

1 In the table below, each row contains three statements about a particular reading skill. Select one statement from each of the four rows that you think best describes your reading skills.

Reading skills		
• Find information in a text	• Select key points in a text	• Use a range of reading strategies to locate information in a text quickly
• Understand points	• Infer meaning	• Identify different layers of meaning
• Give my opinion	• Develop opinions by giving examples from the text	• Evaluate the text using precise references
• Describe some features of a review	• Explain the effect of the writer's choice of features of a review	• Contrast how writers have adapted the text type features to suit the audience

2 Working with a partner, explain your evidence for each statement you have chosen.

3 Working with the same partner, choose one of the reading skills and identify what you need to do to develop that skill further. Write down your decisions and set a date for a review of your progress towards this target.

Imagine, Explore, Entertain

Imagine, Explore, Entertain

Getting started
Unit 10 Structure a story

Your challenge is to write the opening of a ghost story.

◆ The story should be in a bright, modern setting, such as a supermarket or school. Don't use a churchyard, haunted house or abandoned building.

◆ You should use the past tense.

◆ You could write in the first person (I), second person (you), or third person (she, he).

To get you started, look at these two examples of opening sentences and write down what you like and dislike about each one.

It was foggy around the supermarket and I was really scared.

As you walked across to the frozen meat section, you didn't realize I was watching you, did you?

Now write the opening three sentences of your own story. Aim to make them dramatic and attention grabbing.

Unit 11 Portray character

There are many ways to tell a story and to introduce your main characters. For example, the story of Little Red Riding Hood could be told through description, plot or dialogue.

1 Read these three possible starting points to the story of Little Red Riding Hood.

Description	**Plot**	**Dialogue**
As the mist lifted, the morning sun began to warm the forest that lay around Little Red Riding Hood's cottage …	Today, Little Red Riding Hood would go and see Grandma. She got changed, packed a hamper of food, and set off into the forest …	'You will be careful out there, won't you dear?' 'Yes, mother,' replied Little Red Riding Hood wearily. Her mother kissed her forehead. 'Well, maybe I worry too much …' 'I've done it hundreds of times before, you know …'

2 With a partner, answer these questions:

    a Which opening do you like most? Explain why.

    b Which opening grabs the reader's attention most effectively? Explain why.

3 Now think about how you might start the story of Goldilocks and the three bears. Try writing one or two sentences to test out whether description, plot or dialogue would make the most effective beginning.

Unit 12 Narrative devices

Why are some books difficult to 'get into', while others hook us from the first page?

1 Working in a small group, create a spider diagram of the essential ingredients for involving the reader in a story. For each ingredient, write down an example of a novel you have read that does this.

2 In your group, try to agree on:

    a the most successful technique for getting the reader involved from the start

    b the novel that best captures the reader's interest.

Unit 13 Language effects

1 Words often trigger pictures in our minds. Look at the words and phrases below and do some quick sketches, cartoons or doodles to show the image that each one triggers.

disappointment	*bright ideas*	*distant memories*
hope	*dark thoughts*	

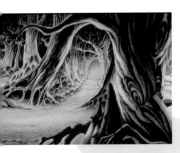

2 Compare your responses with your partner's.

3 Look at the picture on the left. Write continuously for two minutes the ideas, words and phrases that come into your mind when you look at the picture. (You don't have to write in complete sentences.)

Now share your words and images with other students. How similar or different were your responses?

Story openings

Something

Learning objectives

These are the objectives you will be studying:

- Word level: explore words in their context

- Sentence level: explore features of paragraphs; increase the variety of sentences you use

- Reading: explore setting, character and mood; explore writers' language choices

- Writing: explore story structure; explore characterization; use a range of narrative devices

Introduction

Fiction writers often try to grab the reader's attention from the very start. They think of an arresting opening – something that makes us keen to read on – and then put twists and turns in the plot to keep our interest.

Many fiction texts use suspense to hold the reader's interest. We find this most in horror and ghost stories and in thrillers. To create suspense, the author gives hints and suggestions that a character faces danger, but keeps us waiting to see what happens.

This opening sequence from a horror story by Joan Aiken shows how one writer tries to capture and hold the reader's attention. The narrator is a young boy.

Glossary

fusillade – *volley of shots, like lots of guns being fired at once*

gentian – *small flower*

Something

When the thing happened for the first time I was digging up wild lilies to plant in my own little garden. Digging up wild lilies. A happy task. They are dark orange and grow down by the narrow shallow brook that freezes solid in winter. On that day it was babbling and murmuring placidly and I sang a song, which I made up as I went along, to keep company with its murmur. 'Wild lilies I find, wild lilies I bring, wild lilies, wild lilies, to flower in the spring.' Overhead the alder trees arched, and water-birds, becoming used to my harmless presence, called their short gargling answers. Once or twice a kingfisher flashed. There were trout in the water, but only tiny ones; I could feel them brush against my bare legs every now and then as I waded knee-deep along the course of the brook, which made an easier route than the tangled banks.

At the end of a whole afternoon spent in this manner my mind felt bare, washed clean, like the stones in the brook.

And then – suddenly: fear. Where did it come from? I had no means of knowing. *Menace.* Cold fear was all around me – in the dark arch of the trees, the tunnel they made (into which the stream vanished), the sharp croak of birds, the icy grip of the water on my calves, the gritty scour of mud on my grimed and scraped hands. But, most of all, in my own mind, as if, down at the back of it, stood something hidden, watchful, *waiting*. In another minute I would *see* it and know what it was. In another minute I would go mad from terror.

Frenzied with haste to be away from there I scrambled up the bank, snatching my trowel and the wooden bucket in which I had been putting my lily roots – dropping half of them; panic-stricken, never looking back, I thrust and battered a track through alders and brambles, tearing my shirt, scratching my arms and face. Mother would be furious, but I never gave that a thought. All my need was to get home – home – home to Grandfather's comforting presence.

Barefoot I ran over the ploughed field, stubbing my toes on flints, reckless of sharp stubble-ends and dry thistles with their lancing spines. Tonight I would need to spend hours squeezing them out, painfully one by one. Tonight was not now. Now if I did not find Grandfather I would die of fear.

Luckily he was always to be found in the same place: placid on a backless chair with his dog Flag beside him, outside the smithy where my uncles Josef and Willi clanked on the anvil and roared on the bellows. A great grey cart-horse waited patiently, one hoof tipped forward. A cone of fire burned bright in the dim forge, and there was Uncle Josef in his black leather apron, holding the gold and blazing shoe in his long tongs. For once I didn't wait and watch. I ran and clung tight to Grandfather. He felt frail and bony, and smelt, as always, of straw and old-man's-odour, and sweet tobacco.

'Grandfather – Grandfather – ' I gulped.

Holding me in thin strong hands he looked at me long and shrewdly with his faded shrunken eyes.

'So it's happened, has it?'

'Yes. Yes. It has. But what *is* it, Grandfather? *What* has happened?'

'Easy. Easy!' He soothed me with his voice as if I had been a panicky foal. 'It was bound to come. It always does. Your father – your brothers – now you. All our family. It always happens, sooner or later.'

'But what? But what?'

A terrific fusillade of clangs came from the forge. Uncle Josef had the shoe back on the anvil and was reshaping it with powerful blows of his hammer. A fan of sparks rained out, making the cart-horse stamp and whinny.

'Come along,' said my grandfather. 'We'll walk to the church.' He put his hand on my shoulder to hoist himself into a walking position, then kept it there, for balance. He was very stooped, and walked with a limp; still, for his years, he was as strong as an old root.

We went slowly along the village street. Marigolds blazed, nasturtiums climbed up the sides of the ancient timbered houses. Apples on the trees were almost ripe. The sky, though cloudless and blue as a gentian, was covered with a light haze; in the mornings and evenings now, mist lay thick in the valley. It was September.

'Winter is coming,' said my grandfather.

'Yes, Grandfather.'

'Winter is a kind of night,' he said. 'For months we are prisoners here in the village. As, at night, we are shut in our homes. The next village is a world's end away.'

It was true. Our village lies in a deep valley. Often in winter the roads are blocked with snow for weeks, sometimes for months. Up to now I had never minded this. It was good fun, being closed away from the world. We had huge stacks of firewood – cellars full of wine and flour. The cows and sheep were stabled safely. We had dried fruits, stored apples, fiddles, music, jokes, and a few books. We had each other. What more did we need? Up to now I had loved the winter. But at this moment I shivered, as I pictured miles of gale-scoured hills, the snow sent by wind into long curving drifts, with never a human footprint. Darkness over the mountains for thirteen hours, from sunset to sunrise.

'Night is a kind of death,' said my grandfather. And then: 'You know that I have bad dreams.'

Indeed I *did*. His yells when he woke from one of those legendary dreams were terrible to hear; they almost made the blood run backwards in your veins. Yet he would never tell us what the dreams had been about; he would sit (once he was awake) white, panting, shaking, gasping, by his bed; sometimes he might have hurled himself right out of his cot, an arm's length away from it, and, next day, would be covered in black bruises, and his eyes sunken in deep grey hollows.

Joan Aiken

UNDERSTANDING THE TEXT

1 The first paragraph sets the scene. Where does the story take place?

2 What time of day is it?

3 In paragraph 3 the narrator feels fear. What is it that is frightening him?

4 Why does he decide to run to his grandfather's house?

5 What is surprising about the grandfather's reaction when the narrator arrives at his house?

INTERPRETING THE TEXT

6 A good horror story will create a feeling of suspense. How does the title of this story begin to do this?

7 Look more closely at the first paragraph. Compare the first sentence with the rest of the paragraph. How does the writer gain and then hold the reader's interest here?

8 What do we learn from the story about the character of the boy who narrates the story? Look at how he is presented by the writer:

- ◆ in what he does

- ◆ in his relationship with his grandfather.

Try to find three key points about the boy's character.

9 What do you learn from the story about the place where the boy lives? Does it feel similar to or different from your own environment?

10 Story writers have to put across moods strongly. How does the writer make the grandfather's dreams seem so chilling?

11 At the beginning of the story, it is not clear *when* the events are set. But hints build up about this through the extract. Find four clues that the story is set in the past.

LANGUAGE AND STRUCTURE

1 Look more closely at how the author uses language to build suspense.

The writer structures the start of her story like this:

Paragraph 1: focus on the setting (except for the first sentence)
Paragraph 2: the narrator feels calm
Paragraph 3: the narrator feels sudden fear
Paragraph 4: the narrator begins to run

a Why do you think after the first sentence the writer has two paragraphs in which everything seems 'normal'?

b Look at paragraph 3: how does it seem different in style from the two paragraphs before it?

> ## Hint
> • Look at the types of sentences, their length and structure.

c Look at the verbs used in paragraph 4: *scrambled, snatching, dropping, thrust, tearing, scratching.* What do these verbs have in common, and why do you think the writer uses them?

2 Look at the second half of the story. It uses many abstract nouns, such as *winter, night, darkness, dreams.* But in the last paragraph the tone is much more urgent and the vocabulary more immediate: *blood, veins, panting, shaking, gasping, hurled, bruises.*

How does all of this build up the sense of suspense? Start your answer like this:

a The abstract nouns (*winter, night, darkness, dreams*) create a feeling of …

b The last paragraph is very different. It …

3 Horror writers often hold back information to keep us reading. How does this writer do so? What kinds of questions were you asking as you read the story?

a Write down two questions which might be in a reader's mind at the end of the first paragraph.

b Write down two questions that the reader might ask at the end of the extract.

Questions might start like this:

- Why did the boy …?
- Where does …?
- Why was the grandfather …?

WRITING ACTIVITY

The story is told in a first-person style. The writer tells the story using pronouns like I and me. It would be possible to retell the story in a number of other styles:

A **third-person** style would tell the story using he and they.

Example: *When the thing happened for the first time he was digging up wild lilies to plant in his own little garden.*

A **second-person** style would tell it using the pronoun you.

Example: *When the thing happened for the first time you were digging up wild lilies to plant in your own little garden.*

The story could also be retold using a different form – as a letter (from the boy to the grandfather, or the grandfather to the boy) looking back on the events; as a diary entry; or as a spoken story, retold by the boy or the grandfather one evening much later.

Experiment with rewriting the story using a different point of view (second or third person), and a different form. Write a paragraph or two, changing the original style, but keeping the same basic storyline.

Write a few sentences to describe how your rewritten version creates a different effect.

Plots, crises and resolutions

Two Very Short Stories

Learning objectives

You will be studying the following objectives:

- Word level: explore words in their context

- Reading: infer and deduce meanings; explore setting, character and mood; explore writers' language choices; explore story endings

- Writing: explore story structure; use a range of narrative devices to involve the reader

Introduction

These texts are two very short stories. Because they are complete, you can study in miniature the way that stories open, develop and end.

Glossary

booty – *treasure*

Text A

Grandma Meets the Axe Murderer

The crazed axe murderer approached the house. Having ravaged the entire neighbourhood, his sack of booty was almost full.

Alone inside, the old woman sat knitting. The murderer raised his blood-stained axe and rang the porch doorbell.

Slowly, she opened the door and peered into his face.

'Trick or treat!' the little boy shouted.

Diane Elliott

Text B

Moment of Decision

She could almost hear the prison door clanging shut.

Freedom would be gone forever, control of her own destiny gone, never to return.

Wild thoughts of flight flashed through her mind. She knew there was no escape.

She turned to the groom with a smile and repeated the words, 'I do.'

Tina Milburn

UNDERSTANDING THE TEXT

Text A

1 Sum up the story in a sentence.

2 How does the writer make the 'axe murderer' seem menacing?

3 How does she make the old woman seem like an innocent victim?

Text B

4 Why do you think the text is called 'Moment of Decision'?

5 Where did you think the story was set until the last sentence? Where is it actually set?

INTERPRETING THE TEXT

6 Both stories avoid using names for the characters. Why do you think this is?

7 Choose the story you like most, and answer the following questions:

   ◆ What did the title lead you to expect?

   ◆ What was your first impression of what the story was about?

   ◆ When did you spot the 'twist' in the tale?

8 Which story is least successful in your opinion? Try to say why.

> ## Hint
>
> ● To give a well-developed answer, refer specifically to the texts. Use examples in quotation marks to support your comments.

LANGUAGE AND STRUCTURE

1 The stories follow a similar structure to many short stories. They both build up our expectations and then surprise us with a twist at the end. Use a table like this to show how the structure of the two stories works:

What the first section makes us expect	How the last sentence surprises us
Text A:	
Text B:	

2 The 'twist' in each story changes how the reader understands what has gone before. Look at the second sentence in Text A.

   a What does it mean when you first read it?

   b What does it mean when you have read the whole story?

3 Text B creates tension by using only the pronoun *she*.

   a How does using *she* build tension?

   b What might the writer have said instead of using a pronoun in this way?

4 Both stories use dramatic vocabulary – words like *crazed, ravaged, blood-stained, clanging, destiny, wild*.

   a Take Text A and retell it using less dramatic words.

   b Say whether the story now has less tension, and why.

WRITING ACTIVITY

Write a 55-word short story which follows the same pattern as Texts A and B. Make the reader imagine one storyline, and then challenge him or her with a very different ending. Your story might start:

- like a love story

- as a thriller

- like a letter.

Choose one of the very short stories on page 125 and make it into the opening of a radio script. Your aim is to grab the attention of the listener through a piece of radio drama. This means that you will need:

- dialogue between characters
- sound effects to help set the scene.

You might start with dialogue, or a sound effect, or you might use a narrator to introduce the storyline.

Here is an example of how you could start your rewritten version of Text A, 'Grandma Meets the Axe Murderer'.

> Sound effect: *wind howling*
>
> Sound effect: *footsteps outside*
>
> Sound effect: *sudden silence; sound of knitting needles.*
>
> Sound effect: *woman gently humming*
>
> **Old woman:**   What a night. Listen to that wind …

Once you have devised your script, spend time in pairs or in a small group rehearsing a performance of it, either for your class or to record.

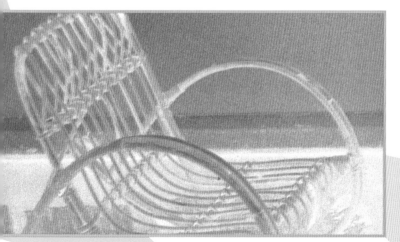
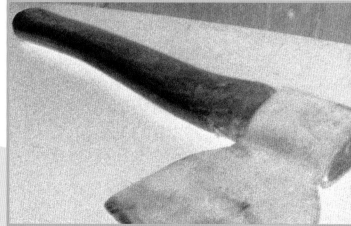

Description, dialogue, and action

Introduction

Novels and short stories tell us tales about characters, often with a focus on just one or two central characters whom we follow through the storyline. The main character of a story is called the **protagonist**.

Writers can tell us about characters in different ways. They might use **description**:

Harry Potter was not a normal boy ...

or **action**:

Harry's scar began to hurt ...

or **dialogue**:

Harry thought for a moment. 'You can't be serious,' he said ...

This unit looks at an extract from *Harry Potter and the Chamber of Secrets* to explore the way characters are presented. Harry and his friends Hermione and Ron are excited to be joining the school duelling club. Harry's and Ron's hearts sink, however, when they learn that the class will be led by the big-headed smoothie, Gilderoy Lockhart. He plans to demonstrate duelling, assisted by the unpleasant Professor Snape.

Harry Potter and the Duelling Club

Learning objectives

You will be studying the following objectives:

- Word level: work out the meaning of unfamiliar words; draw links between words in different languages

- Sentence level: develop your understanding and use of subordinate clauses; expand nouns and noun phrases; use speech punctuation effectively

- Reading: infer and deduce meanings; explore setting, character and mood; explore writers' language choices

- Writing: improve the way you portray characters; make links between your reading and your choices as a writer

- Speaking and listening: work together on scripts

Glossary

Slytherins – *students who belong to Slytherin, one of the four school houses*

Harry Potter and the Duelling Club

Snape's upper lip was curling. Harry wondered why Lockhart was still smiling; if Snape had been looking at *him* like that he'd have been running as fast as he could in the opposite direction.

Lockhart and Snape turned to face each other and bowed; at least, Lockhart did, with much twirling of his hands, whereas Snape jerked his head irritably. Then they raised their wands like swords in front of them.

'As you see, we are holding our wands in the accepted combative position,' Lockhart told the silent crowd. 'On the count of three, we will cast our first spells. Neither of us will be aiming to kill, of course.'

'I wouldn't bet on that,' Harry murmured, watching Snape baring his teeth.

'One – two – three –'

Both of them swung their wands up and over their shoulders. Snape cried '*Expelliarmus!*' There was a dazzling flash of scarlet light and Lockhart was blasted off his feet: he flew backwards off the stage, smashed into the wall and slid down it to sprawl on the floor.

Malfoy and some of the other Slytherins cheered. Hermione was dancing on tiptoes. 'Do you think he's all right?' she squealed through her fingers.

'Who cares?' said Harry and Ron together.

Lockhart was getting unsteadily to his feet. His hat had fallen off and his wavy hair was standing on end.

'Well, there you have it!' he said, tottering back onto the platform. 'That was a Disarming Charm – as you see, I've lost my wand – ah, thank you, Miss Brown. Yes, an excellent idea to show them that, Professor Snape, but if you don't mind my saying so, it was very obvious what you were about to do. If I had wanted to stop you it would have been only too easy. However, I felt it would be instructive to let them see …'

Snape was looking murderous. Possibly Lockhart had noticed, because he said, 'Enough demonstrating! I'm going to come amongst you now and put you all into pairs. Professor Snape, if you'd like to help me …'

They moved through the crowd, matching up partners. Lockhart teamed Neville with Justin Finch-Fletchley, but Snape reached Harry and Ron first.

'Time to split up the dream team, I think,' he sneered. 'Weasley, you can partner Finnigan. Potter –'

Harry moved automatically towards Hermione.

'I don't think so,' said Snape, smiling coldly. 'Mr Malfoy, come over here. Let's see what you make of the famous Potter. And you, Miss Granger – you can partner Miss Bulstrode.'

Malfoy strutted over, smirking. Behind him walked a Slytherin girl who reminded Harry of a picture he'd seen in *Holidays with Hags*. She was large and square and her heavy jaw jutted aggressively. Hermione gave her a weak smile which she did not return.

'Face your partners!' called Lockhart, back on the platform, 'and bow!'

Harry and Malfoy barely inclined their heads, not taking their eyes off each other.

'Wands at the ready!' shouted Lockhart. 'When I count to three, cast your charms to disarm your opponent – *only* to disarm them – we don't want any accidents. One … two … three …'

Harry swung his wand over his shoulder, but Malfoy had already started on 'two': his spell hit Harry so hard he felt as though he'd been hit over the head with a saucepan. He stumbled, but everything still seemed to be working, and wasting no more time, Harry pointed his wand straight at Malfoy and shouted, '*Rictusempra!*'

A jet of silver light hit Malfoy in the stomach and he doubled up, wheezing.

'*I said disarm only!*' Lockhart shouted in alarm over the heads of the battling crowd, as Malfoy sank to his knees; Harry had hit him with a Tickling Charm, and he could barely move for laughing. Harry hung back, with a vague feeling it would be unsporting to bewitch Malfoy while he was on the floor, but this was a mistake. Gasping for breath, Malfoy pointed his wand at Harry's knees, choked, '*Tarantallegra!*' and next second Harry's legs had begun to jerk around out of his control in a kind of quickstep.

'Stop! Stop!' screamed Lockhart, but Snape took charge.

'*Finite Incantatem!*' he shouted; Harry's feet stopped dancing, Malfoy stopped laughing and they were able to look up.

J.K. Rowling

UNDERSTANDING THE TEXT

1 How can you tell that Gilderoy Lockhart is, at first, very self-confident?

2 What hints are there that Professor Snape is not happy?

3 How can you tell that Harry and Ron do not like either teacher?

4 How does Malfoy cheat in the charm duelling?

5 What different types of spells do Harry and Malfoy use during their duel?

INTERPRETING THE TEXT

6 How does the author show the reader that Snape is an unpleasant character?

7 Look more closely at the way Gilderoy Lockhart is presented in the extract. How does the writer make him a figure of fun? You might mention:

- the way he speaks
- what happens in his duel with Snape
- how he reacts to this.

8 How does the writer make the scene comic? Think about:

- descriptions of people
- use of dialogue
- events that take place.

LANGUAGE AND STRUCTURE

1 Look at what Gilderoy Lockhart says. In what ways is his language typical of teachers?

Hints

- Look at the way he speaks to the students.
- Look for any typical 'teacher' words and phrases.

2 Look at the names the writer uses:

Gilderoy Lockhart

Harry Potter

Ron Weasley

Professor Snape

Malfoy

Justin Finch-Fletchley

Some of these names sound comic. Some sound menacing. Some seem fairly neutral.

a Group them into the three categories – comic, menacing and neutral.

b Choose one of the names and try to describe how it achieves its effect – how it sounds comic, menacing or neutral.

3 Look at the language of the charms:

Expelliarmus

Rictusempra

Tarantallegra

Finite Incantatem

a Using the context of the story, write down a definition for what you think each command means.

b Are there any clues in the spelling of the words about what they might mean? Do they remind you of words in another language?

4 Occasionally, to add detail, writers use subordinate clauses to expand noun phrases – like this:

a Slytherin girl **who reminded Harry of a picture he'd seen in Holidays with Hags**

Hermione gave her a weak smile **which she did not return**

For each of the noun phrases below, think of a subordinate clause which would expand it to add detail.

   a Lockhart and Snape, who …, turned to face each other.

   b On the count of three we will cast our first spells, which …

   c Harry's feet, which…, stopped dancing.

5 Look at the way the writer integrates speech into longer sentences.

   a She uses punctuation to show where the speech begins and ends. Write down one of these sentences and label the punctuation, saying what each item is and what it tells you.

   b She finds alternatives for the speech verb 'said'. Write down three other words she uses.

   c Sometimes the speech verb is placed *before* the spoken words, like this:

     Possibly Lockhart had noticed, because he said, 'Enough demonstrating!'

     Sometimes it is placed *after* the spoken words:

     'I don't think so,' said Snape, smiling coldly.

     Write down one more example of the writer integrating speech into longer sentences.

WRITING ACTIVITY

As we have seen, novelists can use plot, description and dialogue to show their characters. What about dramatists and screenplay writers? They really only have characters' dialogue available.

Look at this moment from the novel. How would you show it in a screenplay or drama text?

Snape's upper lip was curling. Harry wondered why Lockhart was still smiling; if Snape had been looking at him like that he'd have been running as fast as he could in the opposite direction.

Lockhart and Snape turned to face each other and bowed; at least, Lockhart did, with much twirling of his hands, whereas Snape jerked his head irritably. They raised their wands like swords in front of them.

You might consider:

◆ using a narrator's voice (e.g. Harry or Ron) to describe what they see

◆ getting the characters to talk or think aloud

◆ using another witness to describe the scene.

You might start like this:

> **Harry:** Look at the way Snape's lip's curling!
>
> **Ron:** Yeah, he looks furious. Makes you wonder why Lockhart's still able to smile …

Working in pairs, have a go at writing this section as a script.

1 First, discuss how you will approach the task, and then develop a draft.

2 Compare your draft with that of other people in your group.

3 Choose one of the scripts written by the group, and compare it in detail with the original version given above. Does it use many of the same words?

Extended writing

J.K. Rowling presents characters by using different methods. She uses description, plot and dialogue. Practise doing this yourself. Take the character notes below and write the opening sequence of a story which shows what that character is like.

Character summary:

Celia Merchant

◆ new English teacher

◆ 40s, small, speaks quickly

◆ eyes wrinkle when she smiles

◆ has high standards, is impatient when things don't get done

Setting:

School corridor, first day of term

Plot:

She sees two pupils arguing and decides to find out what is happening.

Story openings

You could start with one of these story openings.

Description:

The corridor was crowded and the new teacher emerged from Room 23. She was …

Plot:

Celia Merchant heard the argument before she saw it. She moved quickly out of Room 23 …

Dialogue:

'All right,' came a voice, 'that's enough. Break it up.'

Choose one of the story openings above and write the rest of the paragraph. Try to show all the different features listed in the character summary.

Involving the reader

The Mist in the Mirror

Learning objectives

You will be studying the following objectives:

- Sentence level: become more skilful in managing tenses

- Reading: explore setting, character and mood; explore writers' language choices

- Writing: use a range of narrative devices to involve the reader

Introduction

Writers aim to get the reader as involved as possible in their stories. They use a range of techniques, including:

- telling the story from different points of view (e.g. using the first, second or third person)

- using a different time sequence (e.g. starting with a crime, and then using flashbacks to show what led to it)

- using more than one narrative (e.g. telling the interlocking stories of two characters)

- experimenting with tense (e.g. suddenly shifting into the present tense)

- deliberately confusing the reader (e.g. not telling us the name of a character, to keep us wondering who it is).

This extract is from Susan Hill's ghost story *The Mist in the Mirror*.

Finding his way in darkness to his room in an inn, the narrator is about to encounter a strange supernatural presence. Notice how Susan Hill builds a sense of panic and mystery. Use the questions that follow to explore the techniques she uses to keep the reader involved.

Glossary

traverse – *move across*

flailing – *thrashing about (trying to regain balance)*

skeins – *loosely coiled threads*

peremptory – *commanding, bossy*

crone – *old person*

The Mist in the Mirror

The Inn was in darkness. I barred the front door, shot the iron bolts and then felt my way across the hall, groping with my hand outstretched for the stair rail, for there was no window through which the moonlight could penetrate, and no lamp or torch had been left out for me. I thought that by now I knew my way to the upper floors and my own room but at the second landing must have taken a wrong turning, for up here was a warren of short, narrow passageways leading out of one another, and, finding only a blank wall immediately ahead of me, I backed a few yards, before moving cautiously on again. I edged forwards step by step putting my hand out again to keep in contact with the wall on my left. I was afraid of pressing the latch of the wrong door and entering a strange room, uncertain whether to call out, though quite sure that the morose landlord would not thank me for disturbing him.

Then, at the end of the passage, I made out a dim, reddish glow, as if from the last embers of a fire, and began to move towards it, thinking that I might somehow get my bearings there, or at least recognise some familiar-looking corner.

The light did not increase greatly as I drew nearer but seemed to be oddly veiled or obscured. The distance along the corridor was only a few yards, and yet to traverse it took an eternity, I was so tired and dazed.

Then, abruptly, I came much closer to the source of the light, and at the same moment, missed my footing on the single step that was in my way. I reached out my arm, flailing, to save myself and just managed to do so, but I reeled nonetheless, and my hand touched not empty air, nor any solid wall or door but instead, to my horror, came up against and went straight through a screen or curtain made of beads that clung and trailed about me like skeins as I stumbled, so that I felt them not only on my hands and arms but about my head and face too. The sensation in the darkness was a horrible one, but worse was to follow.

Looking up I saw that the curtain did indeed cover an open doorway and that behind a small, dark inner lobby, at the entrance to which I was now standing, lay a room. I could make out little and my impression of it was swift and muddled, in my own confusion and the shock of almost falling. I saw a round table and, beside it though set back a little, a chair, in which sat an old woman. The glow came from a single dim lamp which stood on the table, its lights veiled by some kind of reddish-coloured cloth. The woman wore a scarf, tied gypsy-fashion about her forehead, and she seemed to be dressed in shawls of some dark flowing stuff. All of this I no more than glimpsed before she looked up and directly at me, though how much she could see of me in the dimness I do not know. But I saw her. I saw the black pits of her eyes with a pin-prick gleam at their centre, and a swarthiness and greasiness about her skin;

I saw her hands laid on top of one another, old, scrawny, claw-like hands they seemed to me; and the flash of a spark from some jewelled or enamelled ring.

It has taken minutes to describe, and I break out in a sweat as I re-live the scene, and yet to see the picture of her there beyond the bead curtain in that dark, redly glowing room, took only seconds, but in those seconds it impressed itself upon my inner eye and my imagination and memory forever, and awoke some deep, fearful response within me.

I do not know whether I cried out, I only knew that I recoiled almost at the very instant of first feeling the curtain and seeing the old woman, and backed away, stumbling again, wrenching my hands from the wretched, clinging strands – I can still hear the soft slack noise of its falling off me and back upon itself as I fled. But in my haste I fell again, this time against a piece of furniture set back to the wall, and jarred myself badly and, through the noise and my own cursings, heard a peremptory voice and saw a light, as a door at the end of the passage was opened.

The landlord showed me the way back to my room, from which I had been only a few paces, with an ill grace, and I could not have blamed him for that, but in fact I was very little aware of his sullen complaints and remonstrations, I was so caught up within my own disorientation and fear.

I did not come to or calm myself until I had been alone for some time, sitting in the silence on my bed. I had been badly frightened, not by dark nor by losing my way of course, those were trivial matters, but by what I had seen, the old crone draped in her gypsy-like scarves and shawls, sitting at a table in a dark room before a veiled lamp. Yet rack my brains as I might I could think of nothing in the reality of that to terrify a grown man who had travelled alone to some of the remotest parts of the world and seen almost daily sights a thousand times more horrifying and strange. My heart had pounded and was still beating too fast, my mouth was dry, my brain seemed to burn and crackle with the over-alertness of a state of nervous dread. Yet why? I had to conclude that I was not frightened by what I had actually seen so much as by some memory it had stirred, or something that had terrified me long ago. I could recall nothing, though I beat at my brains for most of that night, for I did not sleep again until dawn. I only knew that, whenever I saw the old woman with my inner eye, I started back, wanting desperately to get away, avoid the sight of her face and figure, her look, and, above all, to avoid entering the darkened room that lay beyond the beaded curtain.

Susan Hill

UNDERSTANDING THE TEXT

1 How can you tell from the first paragraph that the inn is old?

2 At first, what does the narrator think the dim red light might be? Describe it in your own words.

3 In a sentence, say what the old woman looks like.

4 The narrator reacts in shock at the sight. How does he then hurt himself?

5 What is the landlord's attitude as he helps the narrator?

6 Why is the narrator so disturbed by what he saw?

INTERPRETING THE TEXT

7 Look more closely at paragraph 4 ('Then, abruptly ...'). What different feelings and emotions does the narrator have here?

8 Look at the way the writer describes the old woman in paragraph 5. Her vocabulary helps us to visualize what the narrator sees. She also refers to other senses. Explore the writer's choice of words under the following headings:

- Words suggesting colour, or lack of colour
- Words suggesting texture
- Words suggesting objects that are difficult to see exactly
- Comparisons (one object compared to another)
- Words that create a sense of mystery or horror

9 How does the writer build tension in the extract? Look for the way she:

- makes the setting mysterious
- uses powerful vocabulary to create a vivid atmosphere
- shows the fear the narrator feels
- hints at things that may happen later
- holds back information from the reader.

Write a paragraph using some of these points, with examples.

LANGUAGE AND STRUCTURE

1 Is it possible to create tension without using description? Take paragraph 5 again, in which the narrator sees the old woman. Try rewriting this paragraph using as few descriptive words as possible. Make it seem much more like a factual report. This means that you may wish to shorten sentences as well. For example, you might start like this:

I saw that the curtain covered a doorway with a room behind.

a Rewrite the rest of the paragraph.

b Now write a sentence or two describing how the new text feels different. Is there still the same feeling of emotion and tension?

2 The text is written in the first person ('I do not know …'). What would it be like in the second person ('You do not know …') or the third person ('He does not know …')?

Take paragraph 7 (beginning 'I do not know') and rewrite it using the second person for the first (long) sentence, and the third person for the rest of the paragraph.

Then write two sentences describing how the text feels different in each of the different modes.

3 Look at the start of paragraph 6. Susan Hill shifts into the present tense at this point:

It has taken minutes to describe, and I break out in a sweat as I re-live the scene …

Why do you think she changes the time sequence in this way? What effect does it have on us as we read the story?

WRITING ACTIVITY

Practise using techniques which hold the reader's attention.

The narrator is disturbed by the sight of the old woman. Imagine that on his way back to the inn one evening a week later, he wanders into an alleyway and catches another glimpse of the old woman, perhaps looking out from the window of a shop.

Aim for maximum tension. Start with the narrator walking, as normal, then turning into the alleyway. Show the evening getting darker. Show the narrator glancing into a shop window as he passes. Then describe what he sees and how he reacts.

Aim to write two or three paragraphs. Try to make your style similar to that in the text by Susan Hill.

Unit 12 Extended writing

Take a well-known story, such as a fairy tale or legend. Think about techniques you could use to tell that story so that the reader would be closely involved.

You might consider the following techniques, described at the beginning of this unit:

- different points of view
- different time sequences
- more than one narrative
- experimenting with tense
- deliberately confusing the reader.

Look at the story openers below, which are all telling the story of Little Red Riding Hood. Choose one as your own starting point and then write the opening section (or all) of the story. Aim for maximum reader involvement.

Different point of view

I was late setting out that day. I got up late and I didn't feel well. It was after nine when I finally made my way into the forest. It was a bright, fresh morning and I was hungry. Then in the distance, through the glades, beyond the dell, I caught a glimpse of someone skipping, someone in red, someone who obviously hadn't been warned to stay on the forest path because I am dangerous ...

Different time sequence

'I don't know how I can ever thank you,' said Grandma, as she finished washing her face. She looked at me and held out her arms. The woodsman bowed slightly and stepped out of the cottage without saying a word. Hugging me now, Grandma became tearful. 'Imagine,' she said, 'just imagine what could have happened.'

It was three hours earlier that I had set off. The sun was shining and ...

More than one narrative

'I'm leaving,' I called to Mother as I stepped through the door.

'Stay on the path,' I heard her shout as I closed the latch behind me. Same every time. She was such a worrier.

Meanwhile the wolf was feeling irritable. He hadn't had a good morning so far …

Experimenting with tense

I remember that path so well. It will probably always stay in my memory. It winds through glades and copses, leads you into small dips, through shadows and bright patches, safe and reassuring, but also a little dull.

That morning I thought most about how dull the path was. It was then that I decided …

Deliberately confusing the reader

Something moved in the shadows. Then it stopped. It seemed to be watching, or at least listening.

I paused. A bird flew overhead breaking the silence. Something rattled in the tops of the trees.

I felt my heart beating faster. Flap. That bird again. Flap, flap. I moved on.

Once you have written your story sequence, write a one-paragraph commentary describing some of the techniques you have used. Say whether you feel you have been successful in achieving the effects you aimed for.

Using imagery

13

City and Country

Introduction

Writers of fiction and poetry often create special language effects. They might use images to help us visualize a scene more clearly – for example, 'the sea swelled like a monster stirring'. They might use patterns of sound – for example, 'I **f**ound the **f**ear I **f**elt I'd lost'. Poets in particular will use a range of language devices, such as rhythm and rhyme.

We call all of this figurative language. It's worth remembering that many types of texts use figurative language – not only stories and poems. For example, you will find alliteration in newspaper headlines and in adverts. Non-fiction writers may use imagery to make essays, articles and speeches more vivid. But in poetry we can often find figurative language used in its most concentrated form.

This unit looks at figurative language in two poems: a descriptive poem written in the 20th century, and a ballad (a poem telling a story) from the 18th century.

Text A

The following poem by Rosanne Flynn describes a scene rather than tells a story. It is about the commuters and other travellers on a train, and the relationship they have with each other.

> ## Glossary
>
> **aura** – *surrounding glow*

The City People Meet Themselves

The city people meet themselves
as they stare in the mirror of the opposite seat.
An old woman smiles at her reflection –
a girl, who's late for work
and urges the train on with a tapping foot –
the crumpled old woman remembers when
her feet tapped to speed up life
but now the feet are tired and old
and each step aches with dwindling hours:
a starched commuter tries not to look
at the broken-down man who cries –
his shallow eyes, pools of hopelessness,
the business man prays that life will be kind
and the treadmill of time will not leave him to cry
in the loneliness of a busy train;
an eager boy gapes at his reflection,
a huge man whose long arms reach to the straps
and smothers the boy in an aura of greatness –
the boy longs for the distant time
when his arms will reach
into the unknown realms of adulthood;
a worn out mother stares across
and sees another woman with the same gaze
grateful for child, but mournful for freedom.
Their eyes meet in silent conversation.

Rosanne Flynn

Text B

This poem from the 18th century recounts a legend from North Wales. It is about Llewellyn, a man who goes out hunting, only to find on his return that his faithful dog, Gelert, appears to have murdered his only child.

Ballads are an important tradition in poetry. They use verse to tell stories, often using rhythm and rhyme to create a strong feeling of spoken language; originally, ballads were intended to be spoken aloud.

Glossary

brach – *female hound*

board – *table*

sentinel'd – *guarded*

sooth – *truth*

chidings – *cries*

Snowdon – *mountain in North Wales*

scant – *few*

booty – *treasure (here the kill from the hunt)*

aghast – *horrified*

besprent – *covered*

suppliant – *begging*

impart – *give*

scathe – *injury*

rue – *regret*

fancy – *imagination*

Llewellyn and His Dog

The spearman heard the bugle sound,
And cheerily smiled the morn;
And many a brach, and many a hound,
Obeyed Llewellyn's horn.

And still he blew a louder blast,
And gave a louder cheer:
'Come, Gelert, come, why art thou last
Llewellyn's horn to hear!

'Oh, where does faithful Gelert roam?
The flower of all his race!
So true, so brave – a lamb at home,
A lion in the chase!'

'Twas only at Llewellyn's board
The faithful Gelert fed;
He watched, he served, he cheered his lord,
And sentinel'd his bed.

In sooth he was a peerless hound,
The gift of Royal John –
But now no Gelert could be found,
And all the chase rode on.

And now as over rocks and dells
The gallant chidings rise,
All Snowdon's craggy chaos yells
With many mingled cries.

That day Llewellyn little loved
The chase of hart or hare;
And scant and small the booty proved,
For Gelert was not there.

Unpleased Llewellyn homeward hied,
When, near the portal-seat,
His truant, Gelert, he espied,
Bounding his lord to greet.

But when he gained the castle-door,
Aghast the chieftain stood;
The hound all o'er was smeared with gore –
His lips, his fangs ran blood!

Llewellyn gazed with fierce surprise,
Unused such looks to meet,
His favourite checked his joyful guise,
And crouched and licked his feet.

Onward in haste Llewellyn passed –
And on went Gelert too –
And still, where'er his eyes were cast,
Fresh blood-gouts shocked his view!

O'erturned his infant's bed he found,
The bloodstained covert rent,
And all around, the walls and ground,
With recent blood besprent.

He called his child – no voice replied;
He searched – with terror wild;
Blood! blood! he found on every side,
But nowhere found the child!

'Hell-hound! my child's by thee devoured!'
The frantic father cried;
And, to the hilt, his vengeful sword
He plunged in Gelert's side!

His suppliant looks, as prone he fell,
No pity could impart;
But still his Gelert's dying yell,
Passed heavy o'er his heart.

Aroused by Gelert's dying yell,
Some slumberer wakened nigh:
What words the parent's joy can tell,
To hear his infant cry?

Concealed beneath a tumbled heap,
His hurried search had missed,
All glowing from his rosy sleep
The cherub-boy he kissed.

Nor scathe had he, nor harm, nor dread –
But the same couch beneath
Lay a gaunt wolf, all torn and dead –
Tremendous still in death!

Ah! what was then Llewellyn's pain,
For now the truth was clear;
The gallant hound the wolf had slain,
To save Llewellyn's heir.

Vain, vain was all Llewellyn's woe;
'Best of thy kind, adieu!
The frantic deed which laid thee low
This heart shall ever rue!'

And now a gallant tomb they raise,
With costly sculpture decked;
And marbles, storied with his praise,
Poor Gelert's bones protect.

Here never could the spearman pass,
Or forester, unmoved;
Here oft the tear-besprinkled grass
Llewellyn's sorrow proved.

And here he hung his horn and spear,
And there, as evening fell,
In fancy's ear he oft would hear
Poor Gelert's dying yell.

Hon. W.R. Spencer

UNDERSTANDING THE TEXT

Text A

1 Look at the second line, 'as they stare in the mirror of the opposite seat'. What do you think the writer means by the word 'mirror' in this line?

2 Who does the old woman watch?

3 Who does the commuter watch?

Text B

4 How can we tell from the first verse that it is a good day for hunting?

5 Write down one fact that shows that Gelert is very loyal to Llewellyn.

6 When Llewellyn arrives home, what is the first sign that there is something wrong?

7 What convinces Llewellyn that Gelert must have killed his son?

8 Why does his child suddenly begin to cry?

INTERPRETING THE TEXT

Text A

9 What point do you think the writer is making about the people on the train?

How do the city people 'meet themselves'?

10 What impression do we get of these people? Are they:

unhappy   lonely   confused   fascinated by others   scared   shy?

Choose the word that you think best describes them, or choose a word of your own if you prefer. Then write a sentence explaining your choice.

11 The poem shows us something about the hopes and fears of several passengers. Note down what we learn about the following:

Passenger	Hopes/fears
Business man	
Boy	

Text B

12 Gelert is presented as an exceptional hunting dog. Use a spider diagram to show his different qualities. For each quality, write down in brackets a quotation from the poem which illustrates it.

13 The poem was written a long time ago, and is based on a legend set in even earlier times. How can you tell? What clues are there that the poem comes from a distant period? Look for clues in:

a what happens

b the setting

c the writer's use of language.

Then write a short paragraph saying how you can tell that both the poem and the story it tells are old.

UNIT 13

LANGUAGE AND STRUCTURE

Text A

1 Look at some of the images the writer uses to help us visualize the scene:

 a *the crumpled old woman*

 What do you think the writer means by 'crumpled'?

 b *a starched commuter*

 What picture does this image create?

 c *his shallow eyes, pools of hopelessness*

 What do you think this image means?

2 The poem is written in just three sentences – one lasting two lines; one lasting 22 lines; and one lasting one line. What is the topic in each of these sentences?

 Sentence 1:

 Sentence 2:

 Sentence 3:

3 Look at the way the poem is structured. If you were dividing it into stanzas or sections, where would you separate them?

Text B

4 The poem is a ballad – it is written in four-line stanzas and tells a story. Stories are usually chronological texts – they describe events in the order they happened. We expect to find connectives which help to move the plot on (e.g. *later*, *then*, *next*).

 Write down three connectives the author uses to organize the plot in this poem.

5 Because the poem was written a long time ago, it sometimes uses sentence structures that are different from those we would use. Look at the examples below. If the text was written as a modern recount (e.g. a newspaper or police report) we would expect these phrases to be written differently. For each, suggest a new phrase that you think might be used today. The first example is done for you.

a *Nor scathe had he, nor harm, nor dread*

Modern version: *He was not injured, or harmed, or afraid*

b *But now no Gelert could be found*

c *tear-besprinkled grass*

d *Unpleased Llewellyn homeward hied*

e *The hound all o'er was smeared with gore*

6 The writer uses different techniques of imagery and figurative language.

a Look at these examples of alliteration:

i *And **h**ere **h**e **h**ung **h**is **h**orn and spear,*

ii *'**H**ell-**h**ound! my child's by thee devoured!'*
   *The **f**rantic **f**ather cried*

What is the effect of the use of alliteration in each case?

b Gelert is described as:

   a lamb at home,
A lion in the chase

Why do you think the writer has used metaphor in this way rather than saying, 'he was like a lamb at home and like a lion in the chase' (which would be a simile)?

c Look at this description of the day of the hunt:

And cheerily smiled the morn

How does the writer's use of personification (presenting the morning as if it is a person) make the scene more vivid?

WRITING ACTIVITY

1 How important is it that Rosanne Flynn's piece is written as a poem? Would the text be very different if it were written in a descriptive paragraph of prose (everyday writing rather than poetry)? Write a description of the scene as if you are sitting on the train. Use the same characters, but add more detail about the train and the journey. You might start like this:

It is 7.40 and the train pulls out of the station. A few people in the carriage look at the people opposite. An old woman …

Then write a reflective paragraph describing the differences between the two texts.

2 'Llewellyn and His Dog' was written a long time ago and you may find parts of the language difficult to follow. How might it be updated for a modern audience?

Choose one stanza, such as this one:

In sooth he was a peerless hound,
The gift of Royal John —
But now no Gelert could be found,
And all the chase rode on.

Imagine it is part of a children's story written in prose, not poetry. Write the passage as it might appear, making it as clear for your readers (aged 8 to 11) as possible.

Write a brief paragraph describing the changes you have made. Comment on:

- changes to words
- changes to word order
- other changes to sentence structure
- anything else you altered.

Describe how your new version seems different from the original.

Take a story you know well. It may be a local legend or a fairy tale, or something that has happened to a member of your family. Retell the story in a ballad form, using 'Llewellyn and His Dog' as a model. Aim to:

◆ use stanzas made up of four lines each

◆ use the rhyme scheme ABAB, so that the first line rhymes with the third, and the second line rhymes with the fourth

◆ create a strong sense of rhythm

◆ use alliteration to make the descriptions vivid

◆ use imagery (such as similes, metaphors and personification) to bring the story to life.

For example, if you wanted to write on a sporting theme, you could imagine you were telling the story of the English football team who, after a long period without any success, get a new manager from overseas who leads them to World Cup victory. You might begin like this:

The team thought they could never win
The stars were all depressed
The managers shared the single sin
Of not tapping the players' best.

The fans were getting cross and sad …

Speaking and listening: special assignment

Investigation

A local journalist has been told that strange events have been taking place at Lord Llewellyn's manor. She or he wants to interview people who may know something about it. Working in role, help the journalist to find out what has been going on.

The journalist should interview Llewellyn about the day's events, and also the eyewitnesses (e.g. servants, other hunters) who might know what happened.

1 Decide who should play each role: Llewellyn, his servants, the hunters and the journalist.

2 Prepare for your role by thinking about what you have read in the ballad 'Llewellyn And His Dog', and what questions might be asked about the events it retells.

3 Role-play your interviews, with the journalist trying to find out exactly what happened, and how each person feels about it.

Assess Your Learning

Unit 10 Structure a story

1 a In this unit you explored story openings. Look at the story openings below. Work with a partner and choose one that really captures your attention.

The rain was beating down fast. I could hardly see the route ahead of me. Pulling my raincoat tight around me, I stepped out into the night …

It was raining hard. The rain fell like nails into a coffin. I put my coat on and set off on my dangerous journey …

Rain fell in dark torrents, threatening to flood our world. I looked out of the window and hesitated, but I knew I could not postpone my hazardous mission. I said my goodbyes, and left. It was a journey I would never forget …

b Copy your chosen story opening into the centre of a spider diagram. Using the legs of the spider, add labels to show your understanding of how the writer uses language. Try to say something about:

   ◆ use of vocabulary

   ◆ sentences

   ◆ point of view (e.g. first, second or third person)

   ◆ tense (past or present)

   ◆ how the character or setting is being created.

c Underline the features you found easiest to comment on, and circle the features you found hardest to comment on.

2 In the extended writing task on page 128 you produced a piece of radio drama. How well did you perform the script? Did you manage to make your character sound like a real person, rather than someone just reading words from the page?

   a Ask someone in your class to give you feedback on your performance. She or he might tell you about:

◆ clarity ◆ fluency

◆ how much you sounded like your character.

b Based on this feedback, what aspects of your spoken work do you think you need to develop?

Unit 11 Portray character

Work with a partner. Look at the story opening your partner wrote in the extended writing task on page 136. Imagine you are a publisher who has received the story opening and has to decide whether it should be published. What would you say about it?

1 Write some comments on your partner's story opening, but don't show them to your partner yet. Use the notes below to help you.

Plot

◆ Is the story clearly explained, imaginative and entertaining?

◆ Does it make the reader want to read on?

Dialogue

◆ Is the dialogue:
realistic   varied   lively   integrated into longer sentences?

◆ Do the characters have individual voices? Are there alternatives for 'said'?

◆ Is speech placed in different positions in the sentence?

Description of setting and character

◆ Are the descriptions detailed?

◆ Are words carefully chosen for effect?

◆ Are subordinate clauses used to expand nouns and noun phrases?

◆ Do the descriptions help the reader to picture the scene?

2 Make your final judgement on the story opening. Conclude by summarizing your own positive and negative views of the story. Give advice on one or two aspects of the writing that could be improved.

3 Now look at your story opening and write your own comments about it and a final judgement. You can use the notes above again.

4 Compare your partner's comments with your own comments. From this, identify two areas of your writing that could be improved.

Unit 12 Narrative devices

1 With a partner, look back at the work you have done in this unit on narrative devices. Make a list of the different techniques that writers use to grab the reader's interest.

2 Work on your own. Look at the writing activities you have done in this unit and find examples in your writing of the techniques in your list.

3 Which techniques have you not used very effectively, or not used at all? Choose one that you will develop in future work.

Unit 13 Language effects

In this unit you have explored two poems and written your own ballad. Complete a learning diary about the work you have done to show how your understanding of poetry is developing. Use these sentence starters to help you.

What I have read

Of the two poems I have read in this unit, I prefer … because …

My views on poetry

People read poems because …
Poets use images to …
Poets use other figurative language techniques like … These help the reader by …

What I have learned

(Answer 'yes', 'sometimes' or 'not really' about each sentence.)

Reading poetry

I can understand the point a writer is making in a poem.

I can recognize and explain figurative language techniques.

I can identify the structure of different poetic forms.

Writing poetry

I can use figurative language techniques (imagery and alliteration).

I can use the ballad form (four-line stanzas, *ABAB* rhyme scheme).

I can choose and organize my words to create a strong sense of rhythm.

My targets

Next time, I will try to …

To achieve this, I will …

Literary Heritage

Getting started
Unit 14 Literary heritage

As part of your English curriculum, you are expected to study a range of texts written before 1914.

1 Working in pairs or small groups, think about the arguments in favour of studying texts written before 1914. Why should students read texts from such a long time ago? What are the arguments against it?

2 Many people get to know classic texts through films. Some people say you should always watch the film version *after* you have read the book. Others say you should treat the film as separate from the book and not compare the two. What do you think?

Influential and significant texts

'Literary heritage' means the tradition of literature that has developed through history. Since the invention of printing, some texts have stood out as more important than others.

Here are a few examples of texts which have been especially important. Of course, a table like this cannot tell the whole story. It is a very small sample of texts; it mostly includes men; it focuses only on writing published in Britain. Many other writers have had an influence on literary heritage, as you will find if you continue to study English literature.

Literary heritage: a few examples

Text/writer	Period of time	Reason for the influence on others
Authorized Version of the Bible (prose)	First published 1611	Changed the nature of the English language. The language of the Bible had a huge impact on many later writers. The style is clear, beautiful and often poetic.
Shakespeare (drama)	1564–1616	Changed the English language and created memorable characters and scenes. He took stories from many sources and retold them with huge power. His language is highly creative and inventive.
Daniel Defoe (fiction)	1660–1731	Helped to invent the novel in English. He created some memorable characters (e.g. Robinson Crusoe). His biggest influence was to launch the novel, which became one of the most important forms of imaginative writing. He influenced writers like Dickens.
William Wordsworth (poetry)	1770–1850	Changed the language and subject matter of poetry. Until Wordsworth, poetry had often been very formal, written in tight structures. He adopted more informal language, and also wrote more directly about personal emotions.
Jane Austen (fiction)	1775–1817	Changed the English novel. Jane Austen showed how the novel could explore the private thoughts and feelings of characters, how it could reflect its society, and how writers could create main characters who were not always likeable.

Charles Dickens (fiction)	1812–1870	Brought the novel to a much wider audience. Dickens's novels were as popular as our soap operas today. He wrote them with large casts of characters, lots of scenes, a fast-paced storyline, and plenty of cliff-hangers to keep people reading.
T.S. Eliot (poetry)	1888–1965	Changed the language of poetry. Eliot wrote poetry that is often confusing, disjointed and disturbing. He led the way for poets using highly creative language to explore feelings.
Samuel Beckett (drama)	1906–1989	Changed the language and content of drama. Beckett's plays are difficult and disturbing. Often nothing seems to happen: people just talk. Even then it is not always clear what they mean. His plays often show that life can seem puzzling, unhappy, even meaningless. His work can also be very funny.

Dr Jekyll and Mr Hyde

Learning objectives

You will be studying the following objectives:

- Sentence level: explore features of paragraphs; explain the use of sentences in older texts

- Reading: distinguish between the writer's views and others in the text; explore setting, character and mood; explore writers' language choices; distinguish between the attitudes of characters and those of the author; explore literary heritage and understand why some texts are influential

- Writing: explain a process with cause and effect; write reflectively about a text

First, you are going to focus on the work of Robert Louis Stevenson. A Scottish novelist, he is probably most famous for his tale Dr Jekyll and Mr Hyde (published in 1886). This is a disturbing tale of a respectable doctor (Dr Jekyll) who has an evil side (Mr Hyde) that causes terror throughout London. In this extract, an eyewitness has seen Mr Hyde trample on a child.

Glossary

sordid – *unpleasant*

distained – *discoloured, spoilt*

ravages – *damage*

Juggernaut – *an image of a god dragged in procession on an enormous cart, in front of which devotees would throw themselves and be crushed*

Sawbones – *nickname for a doctor*

apothecary – *doctor (originally someone who sold medicines)*

harpy – *monster with a woman's face and body, and a bird's wings and claws*

Dr Jekyll and Mr Hyde

Two doors from one corner, on the left hand going east, the line was   1
broken by the entry of a court; and just at that point, a certain   2
sinister block of building thrust forward its gable on the street. It was   3
two storeys high; showed no window, nothing but a door on the   4
lower storey and a blind forehead of discoloured wall on the upper;   5
and bore in every feature the marks of prolonged and sordid   6
negligence. The door, which was equipped with neither bell nor   7
knocker, was blistered and distained. Tramps slouched into the   8
recess and struck matches on the panels; children kept shop upon the   9
steps; the schoolboy had tried his knife on the mouldings; and for   10
close on a generation no one had appeared to drive away these   11
random visitors or to repair their ravages.   12

Mr Enfield and the lawyer were on the other side of the by-street;   13
but when they came abreast of the entry, the former lifted up his   14
cane and pointed.   15

'Did you ever remark that door?' he asked; and when his companion   16
had replied in the affirmative, 'It is connected in my mind,' added   17
he, 'with a very odd story.'   18

'Indeed?' said Mr Utterson, with a slight change of voice, 'and what   19
was that?'   20

'Well, it was this way,' returned Mr Enfield: 'I was coming home   21
from some place at the end of the world, about three o'clock of a   22
black winter morning, and my way lay through a part of town where   23
there was literally nothing to be seen but lamps. Street after street   24
and all the folks asleep – street after street, all lighted up as if for a   25
procession, and all as empty as a church – till at last I got into that   26
state of mind when a man listens and listens and begins to long for   27
the sight of a policeman. All at once, I saw two figures: one a little   28
man who was stumping along eastward at a good walk, and the other   29
a girl of maybe eight or ten who was running as hard as she was able   30
down a cross-street. Well, sir, the two ran into one another naturally   31
enough at the corner; and then came the horrible part of the thing;   32
for the man trampled calmly over the child's body and left her   33
screaming on the ground. It sounds nothing to hear, but it was hellish   34
to see. It wasn't like a man; it was like some damned Juggernaut. I   35
gave a few halloa, took to my heels, collared my gentleman, and   36
brought him back to where there was already quite a group about the   37
screaming child. He was perfectly cool and made no resistance, but   38

gave me one look, so ugly that it brought out the sweat on me like   39

running. The people who had turned out were the girl's own family;   40

and pretty soon the doctor, for whom she had been sent, put in his   41

appearance. Well, the child was not much the worse, more   42

frightened, according to the Sawbones; and there you might have   43

supposed would be an end to it. But there was one curious   44

circumstance. I had taken a loathing to my gentleman at first sight.   45

So had the child's family, which was only natural. But the doctor's   46

case was what struck me. He was the usual cut-and-dry apothecary,   47

of no particular age and colour, with a strong Edinburgh accent, and   48

about as emotional as a bagpipe. Well, sir, he was like the rest of us: 49

every time he looked at my prisoner, I saw that Sawbones turn sick   50

and white with the desire to kill him. I knew what was in his mind,   51

just as he knew what was in mine; and killing being out of the   52

question, we did the next best. We told the man we could and would   53

make such a scandal out of this, as should make his name stink from   54

one end of London to the other. If he had any friends or any credit,   55

we undertook that he should lose them. And all the time, as we were   56

pitching it in red hot, we were keeping the women off him as best   57

we could, for they were as wild as harpies. I never saw a circle of   58

such hateful faces; and there was the man in the middle, with a kind   59

of black sneering coolness – frightened too, I could see that – but   60

carrying it off, sir, really like Satan. "If you choose to make capital   61

out of this accident," said he, "I am naturally helpless. No gentleman   62

but wishes to avoid a scene," says he. "Name your figure."'   63

Robert Louis Stevenson

UNDERSTANDING THE TEXT

1 Write down two details which show that the door at the start of the extract has not been looked after.

2 Why did Mr Enfield begin to 'long for the sight of a policeman'?

3 What did Mr Enfield do after he saw the girl being trampled?

4 What was surprising about the doctor's reaction to the man who trampled the girl?

5 The man who trampled the girl wishes to 'avoid a scene'. What does he do?

INTERPRETING THE TEXT

6 What do we learn about the character of the man who tramples the girl? Write down any details of:

♦ what he looks like

♦ how he behaves

♦ any particular words or phrases used to describe him.

7 How does Robert Louis Stevenson build tension in this extract? What makes us want to read on?

LANGUAGE AND STRUCTURE

1 Robert Louis Stevenson uses a number of images to help the reader to visualize people and places in his story. Look at the list of images on the next page. For each one, try to say what the description is showing us.

Example	What the image tells us about the place or character
(The streets were) as empty as a church	
It wasn't like a man; it was like some damned Juggernaut	
(The women) were as wild as harpies	
(The man who tramples the girl is) really like Satan	

2 The text was written more than 100 years ago. Find three examples of words which suggest the age of the story. Then try to think of a word we might use instead today.

3 What makes the language of this text seem old, rather than written recently?

Choose one sentence that has a different feel from the way we might write it today. Using two columns, write your chosen sentence in column 1 and then in column 2 write the sentence as we might write it today.

Underneath, write a few lines to explain your changes. Say something about:

♦ how you have altered the structure of the sentence

♦ any words you have added or deleted

♦ any changes you have made to the punctuation of the sentence.

4 Novels written in the past often use longer paragraphs than we do today. If you were editing this text for a modern audience, where would you divide it into new paragraphs?

a How many paragraphs would you have overall?

b Using the line numbers at the side, say where you would start each new paragraph (e.g. line 8 after 'distained') and why (e.g. There is a new topic – the people around the door rather than the door itself).

5 One of the influential features of Robert Louis Stevenson's style is the way he uses different layers of storytelling. He tells the story of the man trampling the child through the eyes of a witness – Mr Enfield. This means that we get Mr Enfield's opinion, rather than simply a description of what happened.

Look at these two examples:

a *He was perfectly cool and made no resistance, but gave me one look, so ugly that it brought out the sweat on me like running …*

b *I never saw a circle of such hateful faces; and there was the man in the middle, with a kind of black sneering coolness – frightened too, I could see that – but carrying it off, sir, really like Satan.*

For each example, say what we learn about the man, and what we learn about Enfield's attitude to him.

The man who tramples the girl	The character of Enfield
a	
b	

WRITING ACTIVITY

By the end of this extract we are clearly supposed to dislike the man who tramples the child. How does the writer make us dislike him?

Write a paragraph explaining how the writer shapes our response. You should aim to mention:

◆ what the man does

◆ the way he is described

◆ the setting

◆ use of emotive words to create a sense of fear or repulsion

◆ the way the scene is presented through Mr Enfield's eyes.

Try to write your paragraph in a way that will be useful and interesting for other readers of Robert Louis Stevenson's text. Aim to build up your argument logically, giving quotations to show how the writer achieves his effects.

The Highwayman

Learning objectives

You will be studying the following objectives:

● Sentence level: explain the use of sentences in older texts

● Reading: identify the main ideas in a text; infer and deduce meanings; explore setting, character and mood; explore writers' language choices

● Writing: make links between your choices as a reader and a writer

Now you are going to explore a poem by Alfred Noyes which was written in 1905, but is set in an earlier time when people travelled on horseback and by coach, and highwaymen were an ever-present threat. A highwayman robbed travellers as they were travelling along the roads and highways of England.

Before reading

Think about what you know about the era of highwaymen. What did highwaymen do? How were they treated when caught?

Here are some starting points for your knowledge.

In the 17th and 18th centuries, roads in England were very dangerous. Travellers on horseback and especially in carriages provided rich pickings for highwaymen. The best known of these is Dick Turpin, who roamed as far afield as Buckinghamshire, Essex and Yorkshire. He was born – and later hanged and buried – in York.

Although highwaymen were criminals, they sometimes had a glamorous and even romantic reputation. For example, the French highwayman Claude Duval was famed for his good manners; it is said that he once insisted on dancing with the wife of a man he had just robbed.

Being a highwayman was a dangerous business, and few survived beyond their early twenties.

As a research project you might use the prompts below to develop your understanding of highwaymen further.

1 Find out the names and backgrounds of other highwaymen.

2 How did travellers attempt to protect themselves?

3 Which roads and areas were the most dangerous?

4 What punishment did highwaymen receive?

Glossary

doe-skin – rabbit skin

rapier – sword

ostler – someone who looks after horses

harry – to harass or pester

King George – King of England

The Highwayman

Part One

[I]

The wind was a torrent of darkness among the gusty trees,
The moon was a ghostly galleon tossed upon cloudy seas,
The road was a ribbon of moonlight, over the purple moor,
And the highwayman came riding –
     Riding – riding –
The highwayman came riding, up to the old inn-door.

[II]

He'd a French cocked-hat on his forehead, a bunch of lace at his chin,
A coat of the claret velvet, and breeches of brown doe-skin;
They fitted with never a wrinkle: his boots were up to the thigh!
And he rode with a jewelled twinkle,
     His pistol butts a-twinkle,
His rapier hilt a-twinkle, under the jewelled sky.

[III]

Over the cobbles he clattered and clashed in the dark inn-yard,
And he tapped with his whip on the shutters, but all was locked and barred;
He whistled a tune to the window, and who should be waiting there
But the landlord's black-eyed daughter,
     Bess, the landlord's daughter,
Plaiting a dark red love-knot into her long black hair.

[IV]

And dark in the old inn-yard a stable-wicket creaked
Where Tim the ostler listened; his face was white and peaked;
His eyes were hollows of madness, his hair like mouldy hay,
But he loved the landlord's daughter,
     The landlord's red-lipped daughter;
Dumb as a dog he listened, and he heard the robber say –

[V]

"One kiss, my bonny sweetheart, I'm after a prize to-night,
But I shall be back with the yellow gold before the morning light;
Yet, if they press me sharply, and harry me through the day,
Then look for me by moonlight,
     Watch for me by moonlight,
I'll come to thee by moonlight, though hell should bar the way.

[VI]

He rose upright in the stirrups; he scarce could reach her hand,
But she loosened her hair i' the casement! His face burnt like a brand
As the black cascade of perfume came tumbling over his breast;
And he kissed its waves in the moonlight,
     (Oh, sweet black waves in the moonlight!)
Then he tugged at his rein in the moonlight, and galloped away to the west.

Part Two

[I]

He did not come in the dawning; he did not come at noon;
And out o' the tawny sunset, before the rise o' the moon,
When the road was a gipsy's ribbon, looping the purple moor,
A red-coat troop came marching –
     Marching – marching –
King George's men came marching, up to the old inn-door.

[II]

They said no word to the landlord, they drank his ale instead,
But they gagged his daughter and bound her to the foot of her narrow bed;
Two of them knelt at her casement, with muskets at their side!
There was death at every window;
     And hell at one dark window;
For Bess could see, through the casement, the road that *he* would ride.

[III]

They had tied her up to attention, with many a sniggering jest;
They bound a musket beside her, with the barrel beneath her breast!
'Now keep good watch!' and they kissed her.
She heard the dead man say –
Look for me by moonlight;
     Watch for me by moonlight;
I'll come to thee by moonlight, though hell should bar the way!

[IV]

She twisted her hands behind her; but all the knots held good!
She writhed her hands till her fingers were wet with sweat or blood!
They stretched and strained in the darkness, and the hours crawled by like
    years,
Till, now, on the stroke of midnight,
     Cold, on the stroke of midnight,
The tip of one finger touched it! The trigger at least was hers!

[V]

The tip of one finger touched it; she strove no more for the rest!
Up, she stood up to attention, with the barrel beneath her breast,
She would not risk their hearing; she would not strive again;
For the road lay bare in the moonlight;
     Blank and bare in the moonlight;
And the blood of her veins in the moonlight throbbed to her love's refrain.

[VI]

Tlot-tlot; tlot-tlot! Had they heard it? The horse-hoofs ringing clear;
Tlot-tlot, tlot-tlot, in the distance? Were they deaf that they did not hear?
Down the ribbon of moonlight, over the brow of the hill,
The highwayman came riding,
     Riding, riding!
The red-coats looked to their priming! She stood up straight and still!

[VII]

Tlot-tlot, in the frosty silence! *Tlot-tlot*, in the echoing night!
Nearer he came and nearer! Her face was like a light!
Her eyes grew wide for a moment; she drew one last deep breath,
Then her finger moved in the moonlight,
      Her musket shattered the moonlight,
Shattered her breast in the moonlight and warned him – with her death.

[VIII]

He turned; he spurred to the westward; he did not know who stood
Bowed, with her head o'er the musket, drenched with her own red blood!
Not till the dawn he heard it, his face slowly blanched to hear
How Bess, the landlord's daughter,
      The landlord's black-eyed daughter,
Had watched for her love in the moonlight, and died in the darkness there.

[IX]

Back, he spurred like a madman, shrieking a curse to the sky,
With the white road smoking behind him and his rapier brandished high!
Blood-red were his spurs i' the golden noon; wine-red was his velvet coat,
When they shot him down on the highway,
      Down like a dog on the highway,
And he lay in his blood on the highway, with a bunch of lace at his throat.

*   *   *   *   *   *

[X]

And still of a winter's night, they say, when the wind is in the trees,
When the moon is a ghostly galleon tossed upon cloudy seas,
When the road is a ribbon of moonlight over the purple moor,
A highwayman comes riding –
      Riding – riding –
A highwayman comes riding, up to the old inn-door.

[XI]

Over the cobbles he clatters and clangs in the dark inn-yard,
And he taps with his whip on the shutters, but all is locked and barred;
He whistles a tune to the window, and who should be waiting there
But the landlord's black-eyed daughter,
      Bess, the landlord's daughter,
Plaiting a dark red love-knot into her long black hair.

Alfred Noyes

UNDERSTANDING THE TEXT

1 Draw a quick sketch to show what the highwayman looks like, according to the poem. Focus on what he wears and what he carries with him. Use arrows and labels to make your sketch clearer.

2 Now do the same for Bess, the landlord's daughter.

3 What is the basic storyline of the poem? Draw a flow diagram showing the main stages of what happens. Aim to have five to eight main events.

4 Both the highwayman and Bess die at the end of the poem. How do they die?

INTERPRETING THE TEXT

5 Is the highwayman a hero or villain in this poem? What are we supposed to admire about him? What are his faults? Scan the text for any clues and complete a chart like the one below.

Admirable qualities	Faults

6 What are the final two stanzas of the poem about? How do you explain them?

7 Which of these statements do you think best sums up the theme of the poem? Explain your choice.

   a It is about love.

   b It is about loyalty.

   c It shows us that even villains can have good qualities.

   d It shows us that even attractive people can be villains.

   e It is about the dangers of England's roads in the past.

LANGUAGE AND STRUCTURE

1 The writer uses language to help us hear the sounds in the poem, as well as to visualize the scenes he describes.

   a Scan the text for words that are aural and visual, and complete a chart like the one below. Two examples are provided to get you started.

Aural (sound)	Visual (sight)
clattered	purple

   b Look at the words you have written down. What do the sounds mostly describe – the highwayman, his horse or the general atmosphere? What do the visual details mostly describe – people or places?

2 The writer mentions colours in many stanzas of the poem.

   a Make a list of the numbers of all the stanzas in the poem: Part One stanzas I to VI and Part Two stanzas I to XI.

   b Reread each stanza of the poem. Using coloured crayons or felt-tip pens, mark any colours you find after the number of the stanza.

   c Why do you think the writer emphasizes certain colours?

3 Why do you think the writer uses so many exclamation marks (!) in the poem?

4 The writer uses alliteration, which means repeating the first sounds of words to create a dramatic effect.

    a Find five examples of alliteration in the poem.

    b Why do you think the writer uses alliteration so much? How does it help us to feel the mood of the poem?

    c Now write a sentence saying whether you like or dislike this use of alliteration. Try to give reasons for your answer.

5 a This poem was written around 100 years ago and is set even earlier in time. If you were a historian discovering this poem, how would the language help you to work out that it was written a long time ago?

    b Can you find any words that we would not use today?

    c Can you find any words that we would use today, but which now have different meanings?

WRITING ACTIVITY

Imagine that the story of the highwayman is being made into a film by the team that made *Pirates of the Caribbean*. You have been asked to come up with some ideas for the opening sequence – something that will really grab the attention of a film audience.

1 First think about how the film should open. Would it begin with titles (names of actors and the director, name of the film and so on), or would you start with visuals before the titles?

2 Now write a paragraph describing the opening scene, up to stanza IV. Write in the present tense and aim to make it as visual and attention grabbing as possible. Use this as a starting point, if you wish:

Mist hovers thickly above the ground. A tree, like a wizened old hand, is just visible, but it is evening and light is fading. Suddenly we hear a distant clattering of horses' hooves …

Alternatively, you could produce a storyboard, adding notes to make sure that the contents of the frames are clear to the reader.

Do some research into English literary heritage. Choose five of the names below (all of whom are listed in the national curriculum for English) and produce a poster or display which shows:

◆ something about who they were (give pictures, dates, where they lived)

◆ something about the texts they wrote (give a list of key titles, subjects, illustrations of book covers)

◆ an extract from one text (e.g. an opening paragraph)

◆ a quotation from someone about why the writer was so influential (e.g. a critic, an editor, a teacher).

Put all the different posters together to create a class display which shows some important figures in literary heritage. You could sequence the display in order, perhaps with a timeline running across the room, to show which writers wrote in which periods.

Choose from the following authors:

Jane Austen	E.M. Forster
Charlotte Brontë	Thomas Hardy
Emily Brontë	John Keats
Robert Browning	D.H. Lawrence
Geoffrey Chaucer	Wilfred Owen
Samuel Taylor Coleridge	Mary Shelley
Daniel Defoe	William Shakespeare
Charles Dickens	George Bernard Shaw
John Donne	Robert Louis Stevenson
George Eliot	William Wordsworth
T.S. Eliot	

Assess Your Learning

Unit 14 Literary heritage
Dr Jekyll and Mr Hyde

When you study older texts, such as the extract from Dr Jekyll and Mr Hyde in this unit, you sometimes find features which can make it difficult to understand the text.

1 Copy and complete the table below, saying how easy or difficult to understand you found each feature.

Feature	Easy/quite easy/ quite hard/difficult to understand	Reading strategy to help
Long paragraphs		
Sentence structures		
Punctuation marks		
Unfamiliar vocabulary		

Then suggest a reading strategy that will help when you are reading other older texts. Some examples of reading strategies are:

- reread the text
- read the text aloud
- break the text into manageable chunks
- work out the meaning of words from their context
- create a glossary of unfamiliar words

2 In Dr Jekyll and Mr Hyde, Robert Louis Stevenson uses techniques that are still popular with writers today. Look back at your work on this text and colour the traffic lights to show how well you were able to explain the effect of each technique.

Technique	How well I responded
Emotive language	○
Imagery to help the reader visualize people and places	○
Describing characters and settings	○
Telling a story from different viewpoints	○

● I can recognize the technique but find it difficult to explain the effect.

◐ I can sometimes explain the effect of the technique, but not always.

○ I can explain the effect of the technique.

The Highwayman

1 Use a large copy of the description you wrote in the writing activity on page 173. On sticky notes, write lines or phrases from the poem and place them around your description to show where you have captured the ideas from the poem. Make sure you include how you would show the sounds, colours, places, and past setting of the poem.

2 Take one of your sticky notes and work with a partner to discuss in detail how you have interpreted that line or phrase for the film.

3 Exchange your description with a partner. Imagine you are Alfred Noyes and you are reviewing the descriptions of the opening of the poem. Write a comment about how well you think your partner has adapted your poem for the film.

4 Now return to your own work. Write a sentence or two to explain how writing your description of the opening sequence helped you to understand the poem.